Break the Rules:

How to Get Hired for Any Job Without Even Applying

Pete Lindor

CONTENTS:

Intro:

Last Year, The Conference Board conducted a study to measure levels of job satisfaction among Americans. They found that less than 50% of Americans report being satisfied with their jobs. This doesn't even take into account if people are happy in their job. It merely measures the number of people that find some satisfaction in their job.

If over half of us are completely dissatisfied with our jobs, many of us in the other half probably still dream of some other job where we will be more valued, have better pay or benefits, or simply do work that is more meaningful to us. However, in this day in age, the competition for these coveted jobs is higher than ever. When you get on LinkedIn and you see a job opening that looks interesting, then you scroll down and see that 2000 people have already applied it can be quite discouraging.

You might start applying for jobs right and left but deep down you believe no one will notice your application or even if they do, you won't get the job because there is so much competition. So you give up before you even try. You settle for mediocrity and resign yourself to your current situation. You tell yourself, "this is as good as it's going to get."

What if I told you that it was possible to get a leg up on the competition? What if you discovered the truth about hiring and interviewing that 90% of your competition doesn't know? They, like you, are probably firing off resumes and cover letters by the ten's and hundreds with similar beliefs of inevitable rejection.

This book will teach you how to make the best impression in an interview, stand up head and shoulders above your competition, and convince the hiring manager that not only are you the best candidate for the job, but that they will do anything to get you on their team.

If you get to the interview, then crush it, the job is yours

Part 1: Landing an Interview Without Even Applying

One of the most common misconceptions surrounding the job search and the job application process is that people believe it's best to apply for a job after a job opening has been posted by the company. Of course, this makes sense to use because we think: "this is my chance to work with this company, they've posted an opening for a position that I'm qualified for, so I should apply." The problem is, that hundreds of other people are also probably applying for that job. Even if you're the ideal candidate, your application may well get lost in a stack of other applications. In all actuality, so many companies now use computerized and automation resume scanning programs that many applications are never even seen by human eyes. That application and cover letter you've been slaving over may never make it to the hiring manager's desk or it may never pop up on the recruiter's laptop screen. This is why you find yourself applying for job after job—applying for any opening you can find, yet you rarely hear back from anyone. Let me tell you a better approach.

It is MUCH better to "apply for a job" when there is NO job opening posted. I put "apply for a job" in quotes because you're not actually applying for a job per se if you're not inquiring after a specified job opening that has been posted publicly. But yes, the best way to contact a company regarding employment is by completely disregarding any job postings or openings you may see. Let me tell you why:

This is Your Best Chance to Be Seen: if you contact members of the company directly, you aren't relying on a computerized system to slowly filter your applications into the right groups so that maybe at some point it will fall into human hands and someone will skim it and consider calling you for an interview. Instead, you're taking matters into your own hands and bypassing the computerized system altogether. By contacting a recruiter, hiring manager, or business leader directly, you're giving yourself your best possible chance to actually have someone review your resume and give you a response. (We'll get into the specifics of how you can directly contact someone at a company later.)

You Get a Better Opportunity to "Sell Yourself:" By contacting the company directly and not regarding a specific job opening, you're opening the door to showing the company why you'd be a great addition to their team. Instead of pigeon-holing yourself into the specific job requirements you find on a job description for the job you're applying for, you can simply tell the company about yourself. You can tell them about all the value you can bring to the business and if you really want to impress them, you can pitch them a few ideas that you've brainstormed about their business.

This Makes You Stand Out: approaching the company from a different channel like this will really make you stand out. Instead of getting lost in a sea of similar applications, you have the nerve to independently contact the company and "sell yourself to them." Chances are, they get far fewer applicants contacting them in this unconventional way. Most others just fall in line with the, "Apply online and wait for a response" method. At best, the most assertive candidates will follow up on their application and try to convince someone to interview them. But if you completely ignore the job openings and job postings all together, you will really stand out. You may beat the crowd: perhaps the company has some openings coming up and they haven't posted it publicly yet. Or perhaps they will be so impressed that they will find a position for you simply because they want you on their team. Worst case scenario, they might tell you they don't have any openings right now but they'll certainly keep you in mind for the future. Especially if you're contacting a larger company, they're almost always looking for quality people to add to their team, so most of the time they'll at least be opening to hearing from a strong candidate regardless of which job openings they may currently have.

It Makes You Really Consider the kind of Company You Want to Work For: when you apply for a job, usually you're not just applying for a position, but you're really applying for a place within a company. The company is more important than the job itself. If you get in with a good company and especially if it's a big company, your opportunities are endless. You can move around within the company, try different departments and different positions and gain whatever experience you are looking for.

Many people fail to see this when they're applying for a job. Often, they don't even give much consideration to the company they're applying for, they simply just look at job title after job title and read job requirements and then hastily apply. If you choose to bypass the conventional job application process, you'll be forced to really look at companies themselves. It will help you find quality companies that do things that are actually interesting to you. This can only end in greater workplace satisfaction for you, and better job performance because you'll be happy with the company you're working for and interested in the work you're doing.

You May End Up Getting a Better Position or a Better Deal Than You Otherwise Would Have: if you contact them without reference to a specific job posting, you're suddenly not limiting yourself to that particular job. Often when a candidate applies for a particular job, they're only considered for that specific position even though there may be other positions better suited for them. If you contact them directly and demonstrate your skills and abilities, there's a better chance you will be considered for more opportunities.

They may take your resume and your information that you've provided about yourself and compare it to the needs of the company and find something completely different for you that you didn't even know about. This is an ideal situation: when the company takes a candidates skills and compares them to the needs of the company to find a mutually optimal position as opposed to a candidate competing with many other candidates for a position he may or may not be qualified for. Plus, you never know. If you approach the company without reference to a job posting, you may be able to negotiate a better salary since they won't be thinking of you as "just another candidate."

There are many reasons why you should bypass the normal job application method but these are a few of the key reasons.

Don't be discouraged if some of your emails go unanswered or some companies don't seem interested. It's great practices for you to work on being more assertive and really promoting and marketing yourself. In time, the right company will be interested in you and you'll be taking full control of your career instead of just throwing your application at company after company and hoping someone will call you for an interview.

How to find the contact info for anyone at any company:

You may be thinking to yourself, well this idea sounds great but how can I contact any of these companies? They never leave contact info on the job posting page. Here's another chance for you to stand out. If you can be a bit creative and use some detective skills, you'll be able to contact decision-makers directly while none of the other applicants will be able to unless they follow the same steps you do.

Step 1: Finding the Company Leadership Team

Once you identify the company you're interested in, start perusing their website. Most companies have a leadership page where they list all of their top leaders in the company. Occasionally their email addresses will be listed here too—but not always.

If you're looking for a job in marketing, and they've listed a "Director of Marketing," or "VP of Marketing and Communications," or some executive with a similar job title, that will be the person you'll want to contact. If they don't list their leaders on their website or you can't seem to find the appropriate person, don't worry. Move on to Step 2.

Step 2: Finding the name of the Decision-Maker

Get on LinkedIn and search the company. A very high percentage of working professionals now have LinkedIn profiles so it's not too hard to find the decision-makers at your target company. Usually you can start by searching the company name. Most moderate-to-large companies will have a company presence on LinkedIn with all their employees linked under their Umbrella.

Example:

- You search: ABC Company on LinkedIn. If this company has a LinkedIn page, it will pop up there. Usually you can verify if it's the right company by the logo and/or the city it's based out of.

- Once you click on it, there will be a link that shows the number of employees they have listed on LinkedIn. Click on this link and you should see a list of their employees. Then you can filter by many different factors such as "name," "job title," "location," etc. Normally I will type in whichever department I want to contact. For example if I'm trying to find a decision-maker in the marketing department, I'll filter by typing "Marketing" into the "Job Title," search box.

- The results should display all the people on LinkedIn in the marketing department. From there, you should be able to identify some of the decision makers in this department. Look for keywords like "Manager," or "VP," or "Director" etc.

- Write down any names that look like they could be decision-makers in that department.

Step 3: Finding their Email Address

Now you need to find that person's email address. Sometimes it's quite easy, other times it's more difficult. There are a variety of ways to go about this, but I'll list a few of them here. Scour the company's website for email addresses. Frequently, they include an email address in the Sales Department tab, or else in the PR and Communications tab. If you go to "Press Releases," usually they have the email address of a PR contact there. If the company does fundraising or any type of charitable work often, they'll have a contact person for that including an email address. If you've completely scoured the website and still can't find an email address, don't worry.

All you need to find is one person's email address at that company (it doesn't need to be the email address of the decision-maker you're intending to contact.) We just need to know what email format the company uses. If you can't find an email on the website, try googling the company and type email address with the company's name in the search bar. Often you'll be able to find it that way. Another option is to check the company's facebook page. Once you're on their page, click on "Posts," and then in the search bar type "email" or "contact." Often, an email address will pop up there. In the results you'll see any posts that have the word "email" or "contact" in them. Often it will be a post about some event or some sale or promotion with a contact email. If even after all of that, you still cannot find any person's email, don't worry. There's still another way.

An important tool for this trick are websites that verify the validity of email addresses. Websites like www.Hunter.io are great tools to help. You can type in the URL of the company's website, and Hunter will scour the internet and give you their best guess as to what the email format for the company is.

For example, the most common email format for a company is first initial, last name @ domain name. So if it's Kathy Jones at ABC Company, and they use this format, her email would be: kjones@abccompany.com. Another common format is First name.lastname @ domain. So if ABC Company followed this format, Kathy's email would be: kathy.jones@abccompany.com. Hunter bases their results on any data they can find on the internet. If you can find the email format, chances are you'll be able to construct the email address for the decision maker you want to contact. Most companies have uniform email formats which means if you can find a few people's emails online for that particular company, and they all follow the same format, then you can be pretty confident that the email for that Hiring Manager you want to contact will follow the same format so all you need is their name.

Hunter also has an email verifier. If you find the email format for a company, construct the email for your decision-maker following that same format, and then you want to test the email address to see if it's valid, you can use the email verifier program on Hunter. You simply type in the email you've constructed for the decision-maker and Hunter will give you their best guess as to whether that email address is valid. Typically they can do a server test which will verify if that's a valid email.

NOTE: sometimes this email verifier simply can't verify the email address. With some large companies, they have big servers that accept any email address format or combination. Thus, if you check an email with that server, it won't be able to tell you if that particular email address is valid or not, but most of the time, the service works like a charm.

Of course this system is not foolproof but I'd say that its accurate at least 80% of the time. Thus, with a little bit of work, you can find the email address for any decision-maker you want to contact and increase your chances of getting a response from them that much more.

Alternatively, if after all of that, you still cannot find a valid email address, LinkedIn "InMail" is a great tool to contact decision-makers via LinkedIn. This tool allows you to message anyone on LinkedIn directly. You don't have to be connected with the person to contact them. The only issue is that this service is not free. You have to be a LinkedIn premium subscriber. However, you can just sign up for the free trial or simply go month by month and cancel once you've found your job. It's a good investment you can make for finding your dream job.

Actually, you may find it effective to still send an InMail message even if you've emailed the decision-maker also. The more ways you can get their attention the better.

Another helpful tip: it's better to find several decision-makers at the company. You don't want to rely on one person to actually read your email and respond. The more people you can contact, the greater your chances of getting a response. I typically recommend that you contact some high level people and some lower level people. This means a few VP's, maybe even some "C-Level" executives, and then some recruiters or HR Personnel.

Step 4: Writing Your Email

Now that you've found the email address for the decision-makers at the company you're interested in, it's time to craft the perfect email that will get a response. Since you're most likely emailing multiple people at the same company to increase your chances of getting a response, you may be tempted to just blast your email out to all of them. Don't do that. Send the email to each of them separately and of course address it to them personally (changing the names in your Salutation).

The tone of your email will depend on the job you're applying for and the company in question. But the following are some tips to help you write that perfect email:

- Don't be afraid to be unconventional. Depending on the company and the industry, you might really stand out if you're a bit unconventional and break away from all the hiring and applying standards you've always been taught. This depends on you and your personal style, but it's usually better to try to be unique instead of trying to make yourself sound like a cookie cutter employee. Recruiters and hiring managers are tired of reading the same exact applications and cover letters over and over and something unique might pique their interest.

Examples:
  o Be visual: include a photo of yourself (something appropriate, but it doesn't have to be the bland corporate headshot). Or make your resume visual and unique. Or make a video of yourself talking. Include

- o Be funny: if you can find any appropriate way to slip some humor in there, go for it. Nothing ridiculous, just something that shows you're a real person and you'd be fun to have around the office.
- o Be blunt: tell them exactly what you want and tell them exactly why they need you on their team.
- o Be Realistic: acknowledge that they may get hundreds of applicants and they may get many emails each day, but then draw their attention back to you with something unique about you or about the way you're contacting them
- o Be personal: try to include at least something personal about yourself. Refrain from making it sound like an online dating profile (ex: In my free time I like kayaking, and watching old movies ...blah blah blah). Instead make it actually interesting and relatable to your work. You can say something like: "One thing you have to know about me is that I'm incredibly driven. Each year I like to go on a big biking trip and last year I biked across the Mojave dessert. It was incredibly difficult but taught me a lot about perseverance. The one thing I will never do is give up."
- o Keep it short and sweet: your goal in sending this email isn't to be immediately hired by the company, but to simply get a response. Thus, don't make it a long-winded

essay or tell them your entire life's story. Keep it short, interesting, and make them want to know more. This means you don't give all the details up front. Allude to a few things they may want to know more about. This will make them want to email you back so they can find out more about you.

These are just a few tips to really nail this email, but you will need to customize it to your personal style and match what you perceive to be the culture and tone of the company.

Hi Karen,

I'm really impressed with your company and everything I've seen on your website. As a frequent traveler myself, it looks like you provide answers and solutions to everything someone could need while taking a trip. Judging by what I've seen on your website and all of the services and tools you provide, this looks like one of the best travel and tour companies out there. I see so much potential for companies like this and the sheer amount of opportunity for growth in the market today.

I'd love to be a part of this in some way--officially or unofficially. My background in marketing and business development for a multi-billion-dollar healthcare corporation has given me a lot of good ideas and I think I have a lot to offer. It would be amazing if I could help you take this company to the next leve in some wayl. I'm really willing to do anything to help--or serve in any area of the business that need support. I just want to be a part of it.

My strengths:

- *Generating ideas and solving problems—particularly as it relates to thinking outside the box and overcoming growth stagnation*
- *Creating content (writing, photography, video production, event and travel planning) and connecting with people and getting them excited about something.*
- *Drawing every last drop of culture, excitement and adventure out of every place I visit and every trip I take*

I'm not asking for any handouts or guarantees from you, just a conversation. I'm taking a big chance writing to you, but I'm confident you will receive this well. You haven't built your company to what it is today without being open-minded as I'm sure you are.

Congrats on all your current success and I hope we can find a time to discuss some possibilities.

Thank you so much!
Jarod

This email is a submission from a guy who was looking to get into the travel industry but had no experience. He just knew that he loved to travel and wanted to be involved in the industry. This is the email he drafted to the CEO of a high-end tourism company. The email was received favorably. The CEO ended up replying to his email, ended up connecting him with the operations manager for the company, and even set up a skype call with him to hear everything he had to say. He is in negotiations with them regarding a potential position with their company.

Of course, this email wouldn't work for everyone and different CEO's and managers will receive it differently, but Jarod's effort paid off and he landed an interview without ever having applied for a job and without any real experience.

Here's why the email works:

He didn't jump right in with, "Can you..." or "will you..." He didn't jump right in talking about himself. Instead, he talked about them. He complimented them in an ingenuous way—not in a shameful flattery sort of way. One of the biggest mistakes people make when trying to find a job is starting by talking about themselves. Most people will eventually tune out if all you can do is talk about yourself. The most effective way to get someone's attention is by starting with talking about them, then transitioning to you by telling them what you can do for them.

Jarod started by telling them how impressed he was by their business and gave specific reasons for why he was impressed and even told them (in a sense) why his opinion matters. He said he was a seasoned traveler so this implied he knows something about traveling and knows what it takes to plan a successful trip and therefore, his praise about their company is more meaningful and ingenuous.

Then he subtly transitions into talking about himself by saying that he sees so much potential for companies like theirs. This implies that he also has ideas for growth of the company. This doesn't necessarily mean his ideas are good, but an open-minded CEO might be willing to hear them. Most companies realize that no matter how big they are and how great things are going, they can always get bigger and things can always get better. Thus, they are always encouraging new ideas and new ways of looking at the problem. Many modern companies also understand that good ideas can come from anywhere—not just the VP's and board of directors. Jarod is reeling them in by saying he sees a lot of potential in their company. This means that not only does he think they're a good company, but he also thinks that they're not as good as they could be and he believes he has ideas for how they could improve.

Then he cuts to the chase by expressing his hope of being a part of it. Notice that he's not asking for a job, not asking for any type of commitment, he just wants to have a positive impact on the company and influence growth if he can. Then he references his background and ties it in to his expertise and the ways he believes he can help the company. He doesn't get too hung up on his background because he wants to make the email about them. They will be able to see the resume for themselves and they can ask him to tell them more about his background if they are interested. Most people make the mistake of droning on about their qualifications and background without saying anything of value or without promising value. You can have all the qualifications and experience you want, but if you don't have ideas—if you don't have passion and drive, you won't stand out from any of the others. You need to connect the dots for them and show them that your experience and qualifications are simply tools that make you better able to provide value for their company, but the real value is you, you're ideas, your energy, your creativity.

Jarod stays humble and makes it clear that he's willing to do anything they need or serve in any area od the business in order to get his foot in the door. Jarod is telling them that what's most important to him is being part of the mission of the company—not about getting a huge salary or about getting a position of power. This is another way Jarod sets himself apart from the competition. He already believes in their mission and "just wants to be a part of it."

Trust me, this doesn't mean you won't get a position of power, or that you won't make a huge salary, but the priority here is to get your foot in the door. Get them interested in you. Jarod was asked to interview for a senior management position with the company even though he didn't have any experience, didn't apply for the job, and didn't even ask to interview. The ideal is to get them to come to you.

He follows with a few bullet points about his strengths. These are well thought out bullet points that are general enough to be useful in pretty much any area of the business, but specific enough to matter to the reader.

He closes with a disclaimer assuring them that he's not asking for any favors. Many hiring managers and CEO's will appreciate your candor if you say things like that. It shows you are down to earth, realistic, self-aware, and that you're willing to work for any opportunity. Jarod goes a step further and appeals to the better nature of the CEO. He says, "You haven't built your company to what it is today without being open-minded, as I'm sure you are." This is a bit risky, but risks can pay off. Jarod is basically calling on the CEO to be open-minded by assuming that he must be open-minded if he's built a successful business for himself. The risk is that it comes across as pushy or as if you assume that you know them when you're really a complete stranger to them. But the benefit would be that when they read that line, it may hit home for them. They may operate by the principle that "good ideas can come from anywhere," and your call out may have reminded them of that and helped them resolve to abide by that principle.

He finishes with a soft close. On your first email—especially if you're just cold emailing someone that has no idea who you are—it's a good idea not to be pushy. Do everything you can to arouse their interest, but don't be pushy.

For Jarod, it worked splendidly. The CEO emailed him back. Jarod and the CEO carried on a discussion over email for a while, and then the CEO connected him with his operations manager for further evaluation, to set up a skype call and to eventually interview for a management job.
Jarod was determined. He was persistent with the CEO and refused to give up. In following up after cold-emailing someone, you have to show them that you're determined. You have to subtly imply, "I won't give up until you give me a chance," and you have to do that without being annoying. Including caveats like, "I know how incredibly busy you are," or "I know this is just one of dozens of similar emails you're reading today," or "I'm only asking for 5 minutes," will help diffuse the tension and make your emails seem less pushy and annoying.

Other Strategies for Landing the Interview

Word of mouth:

This is one of the most useful tools to landing an interview. If you know anyone working for the company or even if you know someone who knows someone, try to get them to refer you. Especially with big companies, this can not only help you land an interview, but help you land the job. Companies put a lot of work into hiring good people, so once they've hired someone they're invested in that person. Many hiring managers and companies believe that good people know other good people. If they hire a good person, they'll be much more likely to consider someone that that person recommends than someone that just randomly applies with no referral.

The other great thing about getting in with someone at the company, is that they can usually find the hiring manager and directly forward them your resume and tell them about your interest in the company. Again, it doesn't matter how well you know this person. If there's any distant connection, try to make use of it. Keep in mind that most companies offer referral bonuses. This means that if Jerry refers Stephanie for a job at his company and Stephanie gets hired, Jerry will get a bonus from the company for helping them find a great new employee. This is great incentive for other employees at the company to help you get in with the hiring manager. Therefore, if there's any connection you have to anyone at the company, make use of it. It could be the difference between getting hired and getting passed over.

Custom tailor your resume to their job requirements:
The longer you've been in an industry, the more you know that job requirements are often bulls***. Companies often copy and paste generic department-wide job requirements onto job postings without much thought or effort put into them.

However, when you're contacting decision-makers at a company don't just fire off your resume without any more thought than that, custom-tailor your resume to the company. This can mean a lot of things, but this will really make you stand out. If you can show on your resume that you have many of the skills they're looking for, they'll be interested to talk to you. Often this means omitting irrelevant stuff. Many people make the mistake of filling their resume with stuff the recruiters and hiring managers don't care about.

When you're tailoring your resume to fit the requirements of a specific company, try to think about what the hiring manager would actually care about reading. Slash anything that's not relevant to your job. Why? When recruiters and hiring managers read resumes, often they start by skimming over the resume. If they see a bunch of irrelevant fluff on your resume, they'll toss it right in the trash even if you have also included all the relevant stuff. It just gets mixed up and jumbled up with the irrelevant stuff. However, if your resume is a concise listing of relevant skills and streamlined history of applicable experience, their eyes will skim down the list and it will be like a check list. They will start checking off your skills and experience and suddenly think, "Yeah, this person looks like an ideal candidate." You're making it easy for them by cutting out all the bulls*** and sticking to exactly what makes you perfect for this company instead of making them have to hunt for relevant skills and experience. Plus, just speaking of human nature, the less work we have to do the better. For the recruiter, the less reading they have to do the better.

Cover letters *&* Resumes:

The Same goes for cover letters, but even more so. This is your chance not only to custom tailor your message for the specific requirements of the company, but also to express what you know about th company and what you find interesting about it.

Many people just copy and paste the same old cover letter over and over only changing the company's name. Recruiters and hiring managers can see right through that. You want them to think, "this person wrote this entire thing for us specifically."

This can mean including specific information about the company or mentioning something about their track record or philanthropic pursuits that really impresses you. This is also your chance to mention any connection you have with the company or any of the company's employees.

It can be something as simple as: I saw that the CEO went to Ohio State University. They have an excellent MBA program that I was privileged to graduate from …(etc.)

This is also your chance to very intentionally connect any "relevant" experience you've had in the past with their current pursuits. The reason I put "relevant" in quotes is because often, your experience is only as relevant or irrelevant as you make it sound. You may have had some minor responsibilities in your old job that directly relate to the position you're interested in. Focus on those. Feel free to talk yourself up and make yourself and your experience sound more important than it actually was. This is not a time for humility. Your goal is to make the reader want to meet you.

Think outside the box:

I alluded to this when we were talking about how to write your email to the decision-maker. The more interesting you can make your cover letter and resume, the better. Of course, you want to keep it appropriate and, most importantly, relevant, but if you can think outside the box you may well stand head and shoulders above the competition.

- **Video resumes** are becoming more and more popular. If you're the type of person that can be comfortable in front of a camera, this may be a great option for you. If they can put a face with a name and experience your demeanor and personality a little bit, this may be a huge differentiator if they like what they see.

- You can make an **info graphic resume.** This shows not only your creativity and organization, but also that you work hard. They will be impressed that you took the time to create that for them.

- On your traditional paper resume, **add a splash of color.** Give it a sleek design. Add a photo of yourself. There are many ways to personalize it and make it more interesting.

- **Include a portfolio if possible:** This can include a spreadsheet, sales numbers, design work, past projects, letters of recommendation, awards, etc. Anything you think is directly relevant to the job that will impress them, you can include in a little mini portfolio along with your resume and cover letter.

Lead with what you can do for them, not that you really want the job or that it would be great for you:

Many people make the mistake of leading right in with why they want the job or how great this job would be for them etc. This is a mistake because the hiring manager and recruiter are more interested in what you can do for them, not what they can do for you. It's great to be enthusiastic and talk about how much you want the job and how great you think the company is, but don't lead off with that. Start by talking about what you can do for the company and specific areas where you think you can really make a difference there. After you've talked about the ways you can help the company, then you can talk about how excited you are about the job prospect or how impressed you are with the company, or how great of a fit this job would be for you etc.

Just avoid sounding desperate. Err more on the side of, "I'm perfect for this job, and you'd be crazy not to hire me." And less on the side of, "Please please please give me this job!! I want it so bad."

Wanting it is not a bad thing—in fact it's a great thing. Companies want to hire people that are driven and enthusiastic, but if you come across as desperate or as if you're asking them to do you a favor, that's a red flag and they may be less inclined to consider you as a candidate.

Give them a preview:

In your cover letter or intro email, give them a little preview of the kind of work they can expect for you. For example, if you have some great idea about how their company can grow or improve, tell them a little bit about it. Don't go into all the details, but show them that you're not afraid to think big, and that you have a lot of great ideas that could help them as a company.

This, of course, depends a lot on what your experience is and what you know about the work you would be doing. If you don't know specifically what type of work you'd be doing and/or if you don't know enough about the company, refrain from giving a lot of ideas. It could highlight your ignorance instead of making you stand out in a good way. If you're a bit unsure of how to proceed, you could always say something like: "I'm very interested in learning more about how your company operates. I am so full of ideas about how companies like yours can expand and grow and I would love to be able to share them with you."

Tell them You're impressed with them: Find a few specific things to allude to and tell them how impressed you are with them as a company. Don't approach it like you're sucking up or giving empty flattery, but approach it more Like you know what you're talking about—like you know all about companies like theirs, and you're impressed with what they're doing.

This is also an opportunity for you to get specific about employee ratings of the company—but only if they're positive. Companies like Glass Door are all about employee satisfaction ratings. For larger companies, this rating is very significant. Current and past employees can rate the company based on a

29

variety of criteria, but it gives you a decent picture of how people feel about working for this company. If the rating is good, and you notice many people comment about something specific, bring that up in your email or cover letter. You can say something like, "In my research about your company I was really amazed at how highly the employees seem to speak about working there. It was really refreshing to see so many people have great experiences working there." Or you can get even more specific like, "I noticed on Glass Door that so many employees expressed how much they admire the CEO. He really seems like an inspiring man and he must be a great person to work for."

Of course, if the rating is poor, or if there seem to be a lot of complaints about something specific, now is not the time to discuss it. You can discuss these concerns with the hiring manager later after they've made you an offer or at least after you've interviewed.

Be bold but humble: There's a difference between being confident and being cocky. You don't want to seem cocky. Some people shoot themselves in the foot by trying to oversell themselves, then the hiring manager or recruiter will think they're either full of themselves or that they'll expect too much money and won't be team players. Say things like: I just want to be a part of this. Or "I'm so eager to learn more about…"

The follow up:

Another major mistake people make when applying a job is failing to follow up. You have to understand and be aware that you are one of maybe THOUSANDS of people applying for this job. Not only that, but the hiring manager usually oversees many positions (not just the one you're applying for), so you can't deceive yourself into thinking that the hiring manager is just going to keep thinking about you as a candidate. You have to make them keep thinking about you. Typically, hiring managers (and companies as a whole) are looking for someone who is assertive and a real proactive go-getter. If you just passively wait around after applying or emailing them and just hope that they found you important enough to reach out to you, you may be missing out on another value opportunity to distinguish yourself.

If you can show them how passionate you are about the work at hand and how persistent you are and how badly you want the job, most hiring managers will take that as a good sign. If you approach the hunt for a job with that type of determination, confidence and work ethic, chances are you'll be able to bring a lot of that to the job front if they choose to hire you.

See below for a sample email of how you could follow up on your introductory email:

Hi Bill,

I hope all is well with you. When would be a good time to have a quick discussion about my ideas for your content marketing strategy for the next fiscal year? I'm very eager to bring value to the table here and it would only take me a few minutes to show you what I can do for you by leveraging my experience and creative expertise.

I'm free any day next week between 3-5, would there be any time in those windows where we could have a quick call?

Looking forward to hearing from you!

Best,

Annie Smith

There are a few reasons why an email like that can be an effective follow up tool.

1. **It's short, succinct and to the point.** As I've already mentioned, no one is particularly interested in skimming through an endless email to see if there's anything that's actually worth reading. Cut out all the BS and just stick with the actionable quick message you want them to actually read.

2. **It's familiar without being informal.** Instead of saying: Dear Bill, or "To whom it may concern" or any of the typical formal greetings, you just stick with a familiar "Hi Bill." And when you wrap it up instead of the "Sincerely," or even "Best Regards" you just do a simple "Best." What this achieves is a perceived level of rapport and familiarity that is subtle yet effective. It might make Bill feel like he already knows you to some degree or that you and he have already been communicating in some capacity. It also

shows Bill that you're a "no-nonsense" person. You're here just to deliver value and not to butter him up.

3. **It's confident.** You're assuming Bill would want to talk to you. Not in an arrogant way, but you're showing an innate confidence in your own abilities that says, "Given the chance, I will perform. I will deliver." Confidence is key— both in winning someone over, but also in performing a job well. Over-confidence can have the opposite effect. There's a delicate balance between being confident in your abilities, but eager to learn, and being arrogant and over confident.

    Over confidence is not a desirable trait in prospective employees and business partners. It tells the hiring manager that you're deluded and that you already think you know everything and that you probably won't be receptive to learning on the job and you probably won't receive constructive criticism well. If you can balance confidence with an eagerness to learn and an enthusiasm for the job, that's a recipe for success. Employers want someone who is confident in their abilities because they will be able to perform well and bring value to the table, but they also want someone that realizes that they still have a lot to learn. If they are eager to learn, humble and enthusiastic about the idea of improving and learning, that's exactly what employers are looking for.

4. **It's specific.** You're not being vague or asking for vague favors. You're not getting ahead of yourself, you're stating something very specific. You're telling Bill you just want a few minutes to talk to him, you're telling him what you

want to talk about, and you're telling him briefly why it might be worth his time to talk to you. When someone reads your email these are going to be the things they're looking for right off the bat: what do you want, and why should I give it to you (what's in it for me?).

5. **You close with a call to action.** You can easily overdo this so you want it to be subtle. Too many people will write a great email, but then they'll close it lamely. They'll sell themselves well, but then they won't ask for what they want. They won't call the reader to action. This usually means that the email will go onto the side burner and they may or may not respond if they get around to it. Instead, you're asking for an easy response, "would there be any time in those windows where we could have a quick call?" You're giving him a real proposal and you're qualifying it. You're not just saying, "when would be a good time to talk?" That question is too vague. It opens the door for them to avoid the question or turn it back on you.

    They could respond with something like, I might have some time next month, or, why don't you tell me when you're free and if I'm able I'll give you a call some time. Instead, you're saying, "I'm free during these times, would you be able to talk during one of these times?" the only responses they can give are either: "Yes, I'm free at such and such time on such and such date," or, "unfortunately next week won't work for me, but I'm free Monday of the following week." Or, "thank you for your interest, we're not interested in pursuing this matter at this time." In a certain way, it subtly forces their hand because you're asking for a specific yes or no answer that is harder to ignore than if you had just left it all up in the air.

Part 2: Preparing for the Interview

Preparing for the interview is of paramount importance. You might be thinking—well, duh… but you'd be surprised at how many people don't prepare adequately before an interview and then wonder why it didn't go well. When I say prepare, I don't just mean print out your resume and iron your suit. I mean doing some in-depth research of the company, practicing difficult questions, thinking through answers, brainstorming about what might be important to this particular hiring manager for this particular job.

There are definitely some basic things you should know about the company.

- You should know who the CEO is.
- You should be able to remember a few of the company's core values and at least read over the mission statement.
- Know how long the company has been in operation
- Know roughly how large the company is (either in terms of revenue, or number of employees or both)

Having this general knowledge will make it clear that you have done your homework. Of course the chances of them asking you if you know the name of the CEO are low, but it wouldn't look great if you weren't able to provide an answer. Regardless of whether or not they ask you about any of these items of information, it gives you the opportunity to subtly show off a little if the opportunity is right. Often you'll here a question like, "What interests you in our company?" This is different than "Why do you want this job?" Yet people often answer the question as if they were asking the latter. They launch into a long-winded explanation of why this job is a perfect match with their skill set and they list off all the great things they're hoping to gain from the job. While there's nothing wrong with that per se, chances are you'll have already made all of that clear in other parts of the interview. When they ask, "Why do you want to work for our company?" they're wondering if you know anything about them and if anything impresses you or stands out to you. This is your chance to show off a bit. A subtle way to show what you know is by talking about the core values and referencing the CEO.

Example: "It really appealed to me that one of the company's core values is tenacity. That's a word you don't hear often and it's something that is so important to business not only to be successful, but to really fight for your customers and show them that you're on their side. I'll tell you it must have taken a lot of tenacity for the founder Mr. Stephens to drop out of medical school and start this company from nothing while still trying to support his family. And now just 25 years later the company employs over 15,000 people. What a legacy. That is a story I'd love to be a part of. This really seems like a company anyone would be proud to work for, and that's important to me."

This is just a fabricated example, but notice how you subtly showcase what you know about their company while directly answering their question and showing them how impressed you are with the company. That answer tells them: you know their core values, you know who the CEO is, you know how long the company has been in business, and you know how large the company is. Any interviewer will be impressed with that.

Job-Specific Prep:

Another mistake people often make is that they prepare for every interview the same way. Just as many people send the same generic resume and cover letter to company after company for job after job, many people don't do enough preparation for the specific company and specific job they're going after. You want to really know what the job entails, what they're looking for, and how you match up.

You should read the job description several times and you should also bring it with you to the interview for reference. Job descriptions are notoriously vague and generic, so don't put too much stock in it and be prepared to ask them questions for clarification. See what you can find out about the person that's interviewing you. If you have their name, check out their LinkedIn profile. See if there's anything you have in common with them. Look at what past experience they have.

If it's a large company, google them to see what headlines are popping up. Read up on any and all news articles both recent and older about the company. If there have been scandals or financial mishaps, apprise yourself of the details but don't expect to discuss them in the interview. Focus on positive things or else challenges that have been revealed.

Familiarize yourself with the website.

Try to understand what markets the company operates in. It's okay if you're not completely correct, but if you've made an effort to understand how the market operates and what positioning the company holds in the market, that will give you a leg up.

Be able to name some of the competitors. There are many ways to find the main competitors of a company. For small companies, it can be difficult. For larger companies you can simply google it or use tools like Capital IQ or D&B Global Business Browser or Hoovers.

Take some time to read up on the industry (especially if the industry is new to you). Scanning headlines and skimming articles can help apprise you of new trends in the industry and new challenges companies in the industry face. You don't have to be spot on with your knowledge here, just showing that you made an effort to educate yourself is the important thing.

When you discuss what you read and learned, don't state it as fact, just say things like, "I was reading that…" or "it seems like a lot of companies in this industry are struggling with…" You can also ask, "Who are your main competitors? From what I know about the industry, the big players are Company A, Company B and Company C."

Posing the information like this shows that you've done the research, but you also are acknowledging that there's probably a lot you don't know and you're eager to learn the inside scoop. Know that you don't know everything—and express eagerness to learn more about the company, and humbly volunteer what you do know about the company—but don't seem like a know-it-all. Say it like, "I understand that you do…." Or "I really like your company's emphasis on…"

Preparing Questions to Ask in the Interview:

Brainstorm a list of questions for the interview and write them down. There's nothing worse than not having anything prepared when they say, "Do you have any questions for us?" You don't want to overload them with too many questions and try not to ask questions that have already been addressed throughout the course of the interview. Normally, they'll take your questions at the end of the interview. You can visibly scan over your list of questions showing them that you came prepared, and say something like, "Well a lot of these have already been answered earlier in our conversation, so that's great, but I did want to ask…" This will make it seem less strange if you don't have a lot of questions, but you should definitely have a list of questions prepared. When they ask for your questions you can feel out the situation and make a judgement call on which ones seem the most important to ask and how many you should ask without trying their patience.

The questions you write down should range from general to specific. There should be job related ones, company related ones, personal opinion questions, industry questions etc.

- **How will success in this role be measured?**

    This question is good because it asks the hiring manager to specifically define for you what success in the role you're applying for will look like. Asking them to define this for you can help to get an insider perspective on what's actually important to the hiring manager and to the company. Often, they'll give you a response you won't be able to find on the job description. The other reason asking this question is beneficial is that you'll be able to measure the answer they give against the strengths and qualities you've already told them you have. This will help you decide if you've sold yourself adequately or if you need to do a little more selling. For example: they could say something like: Success in this role will be defined in Ability to hit monthly sales goals, achieve growth requirements and meet all sales activity minimums.

This tells you that this manager is all about the bottom line. He wants numbers and measurables. This could be an indicator that you should talk a bit more about numbers and tell them about the kind of numbers you've dealt with in the past. Give the manager hard numbers on what sales goals you'd met and exceeded in the past. Talk about contracts you've negotiated. If you were a top tier sales person, talk about how you compared to the other salespeople in your department. This will go a long way to showing the hiring manager that you have what it takes to be successful in the role—not just based on the job description, but based on their own criteria.

- **What kind of commination and feedback will I have with my direct supervisor?**

    This question is more important for you than for them. This will help you understand how much oversight there will be between you and your direct superior. You'll get a decent idea of how much they will be actively managing you vs. letting you fend for yourself. This level of personal management can be a pro or a con depending on what your preferences and working style are. If it's a role that you're not sure of or that will have a huge learning curve for you, you'll want a supervisor that will really be invested in you and will do everything they can to train you and give you all the tools and resources to crush it in your new job.

If you're the kind of person that performs better when left to your own devices and particularly if you're experienced and already know what you're doing, you may be looking for someone that employs a more "hands off" management style. Their answer to this question will not only help you understand the level of support you're going to get from your boss, but it will also help the hiring manager see that a good working relationship with your boss is important to you. You're showing them that you value communication which can certainly only be a positive characteristic in the working world.

- **What are the opportunities for advancement with this role and this company**

Knowing what opportunities there are for promotion and advancement in the company is very important—especially when starting with a new company. I'm assuming you won't want to be stuck in the same role forever—who would? The hiring manager's response will tell you the value the company puts on development for their employees. A good company won't just reward good job performance, they will have specific development plans in place for every employee from the bottom up. Not only will this help you understand what the possibilities are, but it will also show the hiring manager that you're ambitious and you want to develop and grow and always be improving. Employers like to hire people that are eager to develop because they're hoping if they invest in you as an employee, you'll contribute more and more to the company and eventually you may take a leadership role in the company.

- **What do you see as the biggest challenges for a new hire in this role?**

    This is another one that will better help you sell yourself. You're specifically asking the hiring manager, "what do new people struggle with in this role?" This is attacking the problem right at the root. Addressing it bluntly and openly. Both you and the hiring manager know that if you're hired, you're going to be new and there's going to be some type of learning curve. If you can mitigate that curve by understanding and avoiding the most common issues and challenges that your typical new hire faces in this role, you'll already be head and shoulders above the crowd. Companies like to see that you're proactively trying to address the problem.

- **What do you see as the most important qualities for a new hire in this role?**

    This is very similar to the last question, but instead of issues, you're asking for positive traits and characteristics. This is another chance for you to better understand the job requirements and try to match up the strengths you shared with them with what they're looking for on this job. This is key because often people really personal "strengths" and characteristics that are not particularly important to the hiring manager. For example, say that you're interviewing for a business development position and you really are trying to sell yourself to the hiring manager based on skills you think will be important to him.

You emphasize your organizational skills and proficiency with spreadsheets and excel and pivot tables and financial analysis and data collection and analysis. Then when you ask the hiring manager what are the most important qualities for this role, they say something like, "We're looking for a candidate that is great at working across multiple departments at multiple levels of the business. We need someone that's great with people and good at motivating people to work together. Apart from that we need someone that is able to make decisions and someone that is open-minded and eager to learn how our business works.

Now you see that you emphasized the wrong skill set. You thought certain things were more important to the manager than others, but you were wrong. They cared more about people skills, decision-making, and ability/eagerness to learn than about ability to build comprehensive spreadsheets and analyze data. That doesn't mean those skills are not important or even that they won't be put to good use in the job, but it just means that's not the most important thing the manager is looking for. By asking them to specifically outline the characteristics they're looking for in a new hire, you will be able to speak to that directly when you talk about yourself, your strengths and your experience.

What do you do if you waited until late in the interview to ask this question and you've already talked about your strengths and experience and it didn't match up with what they said were the most important characteristics for new hires? The best way to handle it is with positivity. Act very excited when they talk about the skills and competencies they're looking for. Say something like, "Wow I'm so glad to hear you're looking for…" and turn it back around to show how you would be a perfect fit in light of what they said.

- **Why is this role open? Why did the predecessor leave?**

Be careful with this question. Only ask if the situation feels right, and avoid sounding aggressive when you ask it. You're looking for any red flags that may have made the person before you leave. If the department has major issues or the working environment is miserable, you want to know beforehand and steer far away from this job. This question will help you get a better idea of what you may or may not be getting yourself into. Most professional managers will say something like, "She accepted another opportunity that was better aligned with her goals," or "She actually got promoted to a higher position with the company." These are great answers, but if the manager acts awkward or says something aggressive or derogatory about the past employee, that is a major red flag. If they say something like, "She didn't have what it took to be successful in this position," this is an opportunity for you to find out more about the job and about what demands they place on their employees. You could politely say something like, "Oh I see. Is there anything more you could tell me about it just so I can better understand the role and the expectations?"

Then you can just go off of what they say. If the manager goes on to list off expectations that the employee was failing to meet, this could mean 2 things: 1. The employee was incompetent and should have been able to meet those demands, 2. The company sets unrealistic expectations for their employees. If the second is true, you may reconsider whether or not you want the job. Remember, high turnover is a bad sign for a company. If they cant manage to keep employees, that tells you there's something wrong with the way they treat their employees. That should be a big red flag to you; so, if you discover that the company has a high turnover rate, you will want to consider the implications.

- **What do you think are some of the biggest challenges the company faces in the industry right now?**

This is more for your sake than for theirs. You're looking for any red flags that might be apparent. If they say anything here that makes it sound like the company doesn't have much of a future, you may want to consider alternatives.

- **What's the financial health of this company?**

This is a tricky one and may or may not be applicable. Just feel out the situation and try to find out answers to this question before the interview. If the company is tanking financially, you do not want to get on that sinking ship, so just be alert for any red flags.

- **Can you tell me more about the day-to day responsibilities of this job?**

This is another great question to get a better picture of what the role is all about. The job description might say all sorts of things about what the roles and responsibilities are, but asking an open-ended question about what a typical day looks like for someone in this position will give you a much better insight into what you're getting yourself into. In fact, many employers now will have prospective employees "shadow" someone in their future department as part of the interview process. This serves 2 purposes: 1). It gives you a better idea of that the job is all about and whether or not it's really something you want. 2). It gives the employer another metric in which to test you. Whoever you shadow will be making a full report of the experience back to the hiring manager.

It is in an employer's best interest to hire someone that really genuinely wants and will like the job. Therefore, it makes sense for them to be honest with you about the nature of the job and the responsibilities it includes. If shadowing is not part of the interview process, you may want to ask the hiring manager if you'd be able to talk to one of the current employees just to better understand the job. (I wouldn't do this until you've passed at least the first round of interviews).

- **What do you think of the company culture—both in your own experience as well as what you think others would say?**

  Asking open-ended questions like these is a great way to learn as much as possible about the company. The answers will vary wildly depending on who you talk to. You'll want to see: are they speaking positively about the company culture? Do they sound like they genuinely enjoy working there? Ask as many open-ended questions as you can to learn as much as possible.

- **What do you like most about this company?**

  Very similar to the previous question, this is a fun question to ask just to get a better feel for company culture. Plus, people generally like when you ask them questions about themselves, so a hiring manager may be pleasantly surprised when you ask them this. They might subconsciously feel more favorable towards you for taking an interest in them.

NOTE: be careful not to overload the interviewer with questions. Unfortunately, hiring managers, recruiters and interviewers are people and often let their annoyances and petty prejudices influence their hiring decisions so do everything you can to predispose them to like you and think positively of you when they're reflecting on the candidates they've interviewed.

3 things to remember when asking questions in the interview:

1. ***Who am I talking to?*** *If it's a very job specific question and you're not talking to the hiring manager (say that you're talking to the recruiter), don't bother asking. They won't have any better answer for you than what they've already told you about the job.*

2. ***How will this question come off?*** *You have to base this around the vibe of the interview and how things have been going thus far. If the question will come off as aggressive or just annoying, it's better not to ask it. You will just have to feel it out.*

3. ***Is this question going to stump the interviewer?*** *Typically, you don't want to ask a question that's too difficult or too specific that they interviewer won't be able to answer it. Some people will feel resentful if you ask them a question that they don't know the answer to.*

   When certain types of people are acting in positions of authority and then are asked questions they don't know the answer to, it makes them feel insecure and somewhat embarrassed. These feelings can turn to resentment which is the last thing you want the interviewer feeling about you, so just try to feel the situation out and ask only questions that seem appropriate. If you ask a question and they hesitate or seem like they don't know the answer, try to partially answer it for them to take the pressure off.

   For example: "What's the financial health of the company like?" the interviewer freezes and looks like they weren't expecting that question. You

*can jump back in to take the pressure off of them,
"I read online that their last quarter was really
good…" (etc. you get the idea).*

- be ready for any questions they might ask you, and have a good answer—particularly for the difficult ones: Why were you let go from this job? What's your biggest issue or struggle in the workplace? Tell me about a time when you had a conflict in the workplace?
- prepare a great answer for "tell me about yourself" try to make yourself stand out instead of just giving the basic 30 second life story. Don't ramble, keep it short, interesting and to the point.

Interview Questions:

Probably even more important than preparing questions for the interview is preparing for questions that will be asked of you in the interview.

Although you can't prepare for everything here, you can mitigate the risk of being caught off guard by thinking through answers to many of the potential questions that will be asked of you. When people are not prepared for a question, they often get frazzled and start stumbling over their words because they're unable to think of something quick on the spot. Most people are nervous and under pressure in an interview setting, so it's not the best environment to come up with good answers on the spot. As a result, people often give weak or even bizarre answers to questions put to them because they're nervous and fumbling for something to say.

An exercise I like to do is to take a list of potential interview questions and jot down answers to them as if they were being asked of me right in that moment. Typically, I will jot down bullet point answers to each question—I don't write out a full scripted answer, just basic ideas of the main points I would hit.

Why don't I write down full answers? Mainly because I don't want my answers to appear scripted when they're asked of me. I want to be able to verbalize what I want to say candidly based off of points I've written down. Not only do the points help guide you in your answers, but they also make sure you don't forget any points in your answer. Many questions warrant multi-faceted answers that will require you to make multiple points. When the pressure is on, we're often not thinking clearly, and without those bullet points, an important component of our answer that we carefully thought out could easily slip our mind.

Questions:

- **What are your strengths**

  This is your chance to brag. Although usually your strengths will be listed on your resume, and you'll get a chance to discuss them over the course of the interview, when they ask you a targeted question like this, it's good to have a pointed, sharp answer for them. This means picking 2 or 3 strengths that are not only things you excel at, but traits that are highly relevant and important to the job you're interviewing for. For each strength you discuss, give a bit of support or proof for the strength. This could be including an example or referencing something from your resume to provide support for your claim that this is one of your strengths. Do not ramble, and do not go on and on about one particular strength. Name a few of them, provide support, and then you can wrap it up by saying something like, "these are a few of my strengths. My resume provides more details and I'm happy to share more with you about these skills or any of my other areas of proficiency." This is a good way to close because you're implying that not only do you have more skills than what you just told them about, but that if they want to know more about any particular skill or trait, you're leaving the door open for them to do so.

This answer should be more focused on what the employer needs than just your general areas of excellence. Try to be honest, but pick strengths that are highly relevant that you perceive will be the most important to a candidate applying for this role.

At least one of the strengths you mention should be very job-specific. The other's can be more general personality or character traits that are relevant to the job.

Let's say that you're interviewing for an HR Management job:
"I'd say one of my best strengths is leadership. From a young age I was always a leader. As the oldest of 5 kids, somebody had to take charge. In my 5 years of experience as HR Business Partner at ABC company, I managed a team of 6 Recruiters and HR Generalists. Taking on the responsibility of finding top talent and filling the company with quality people is a huge undertaking but I

relished the challenge. I like to lead by example, so I think all my employees would tell you that they knew how to tackle particular situations because they saw me doing it and acting as an example for all of them. It's a delicate balance, managing all current employee development plans while also constantly bringing in new talent and I'm happy to say that under my leadership, we experienced one of the highest employee retention rates in company history.

Another one of my strengths that goes hand in hand with leadership is teaching. There's very little I enjoy more than teaching. There's something so inspiring about being with someone that's eager to learn. Every year I've spent in the working world, I've been building a wealth of knowledge and experience that I get to share with my employees and trainees every day. It's so rewarding to be able to see them take the seeds you've planted and grow into remarkable professionals that will take the working world by storm. I firmly believe that if you empower people with the right resources and instill the right confidence in them, they will rise to any challenge that is set before them. One of my pet projects at my previous job was starting some self-development initiatives. We started having free company-sponsored classes that covered a wide range of topics. Employees could enroll in these classes and expand their knowledge either for self-fulfillment or to help them learn the skills needed to progress towards their career goals. Most of our classes were filled at 100% capacity which just goes to show that people love to learn. Not only did this contribute to the development of our employees, but it also really improved Employee job Satisfaction and I believe it also contributed to our high employee retention rates which made it an incredibly worthwhile investment for the company."

- **What is your greatest weakness?**

Many people give canned or annoying responses to this question. People are afraid of showing that they really have any real weaknesses, so most commonly, they'll say something that sounds in theory like it could be a weakness, but twist it into a strength. While this isn't a completely terrible strategy, most interviewers will see through it very easily.

Even worse, some people are way too honest with this question. They give personal weaknesses that should not be divulged. They panic and say something that will raise a red flag. While you want to be honest, you don't want to be too honest. Saying, "I have a drinking problem." Or "I'm a sex addict," are not the type of answers they're looking for here. Similarly, if you share something workplace related that is an important part of the job, that will also be a red flag. If you're interviewing for a sales job and you say your greatest weakness is "talking to strangers," this will be a huge red flag. A vital part of the job you are interviewing for is also what you're calling your greatest weakness. You want to avoid that.

The most common way people answer these questions is by saying something that really isn't a weakness and then turning it into a brag.

For example, you could say: *My greatest weakness is that I work too hard. Often, I will take work home with me and so I'm trying to find a better work-life balance. I am just very passionate about what I do so the hours fly by and there's always more work to be done.*

While this answer isn't half bad, most interviewers will think that you're just avoiding the question. Often, they want you to tell them a real weakness—something that you struggle with but are working to address. If you can show them that you're self-aware enough to know what your struggles are and how to overcome them, not only will they respect you more, but they'll appreciate your honesty and will probably think better of you than if you gave them a canned braggy response that is so common. So basically, you want to pick something that is workplace related, but not something that is of vital importance to performing the job at hand, and talk about it and how you're addressing the issue and how you're already making progress with it.

Here's an example. Let's say you're interviewing for a sales role and the weakness you decide to talk about is that you're not tech savvy: *One thing I always struggled with was mastering all the different tech and software programs that people are using. I'm not naturally a very tech savvy person. I actually didn't even get a smartphone until 2012. As a sales person, I didn't have to know how to use Publisher or Illustrator or Even more than just basic stuff in Excel, but I really thought that learning some of that stuff would not only make me more well-rounded, but a better salesperson too. At my previous job, they offered quarterly Excel classes. I took an 8-week course where you basically just have 2 classroom hours a week, and it was great! I learned a lot. Now I know how to make cool pivot tables and fancy spreadsheets for my clients. It's helped me get more organized. Although I'll probably never be naturally inclined towards the latest technology, I've really tried to challenge myself to learn as much as I can so I can use it to be even better at what I do.*

- **What were your responsibilities at your last job?**

This is your big chance to brag. No seriously. This is when you really want to lay it on thick and talk about all the things you did at your last job. This is your opportunity to sell it and not just tell them basic things they can see on your resume. The beauty of this is that they will never fully know the scope or magnitude of your responsibilities at your old job, so you can make them sound more impressive than they felt to you at the time. It's all in the delivery. You can make anything sound impressive with the right attitude and the right delivery. The same goes for what you write on your resume, but you'll have to be even more creative in person because they will probably probe and ask questions about it.

For example, if you were working in inside sales and you felt like you were just a glorified customer service rep, you have opportunity to spin it. Perhaps a smaller part of your job was taking on client meetings and doing in-person selling. You can make it sound like that was a very important part of your job even if you feel like it wasn't the main focus. The truth is that it very well could have been the most important part of the job in your eyes and if it's the most relevant experience to bring to the interview for the job you're looking for, then that's what you should focus on.

Let's say Terry works in inside sales for a company where she's an account manager. She is responsible for keeping existing customers happy as well as for bringing in new business every month. She works with businesses of varying sizes and tries to sell her company and solutions to them. About once a month she travels around her territory to meet with existing clients or to pitch new clients. Her company helps healthcare businesses manage their supply costs and supply chain.

Here are some bullet points we could write for Terry to Make her sound more impressive:

- Managed all accounts in a territory of 5 states where I exceeded sales goals.
- Negotiated contracts and agreements with C-level executives at various healthcare organizations
- Forged new and maintained existing long-term relationships with executives at my accounts within my assigned geographic territory of 5 states.
- Exceeded aggressive sales targets as well as personal goals winning B2B and referral business.
- Optimized cost management and supply chain for my accounts through expert consulting efforts.

Terry could also go into specifics in terms of Numbers. She could talk about account sizes that she handles, she could talk about monthly or annual sales figures, she could talk about big wins she's had, and she could talk about any type of awards or contests she's won. The thing to remember is that it doesn't matter how small or insignificant these things felt to you at the time, you can make them sound very impressive with the right delivery. If you were on a small inside sales team and were part of the end-of-year sales contest in your department and ended up winning, you can make that sound like an impressive achievement. My advice is to leave it vague so you're not bending the truth, but you're also not downplaying it or making them think it was no big deal. You could say something like, *"I won the 2015 Sales contest for most new accounts." This is something you could put on your resume too. If they ask you to tell them more about it, be honest and tell them the specifics but make it sound like it was very exciting and you were very honored—even if that's not how you felt at the time.*

- **Why do you want to work here?**

 This is different than the "Why do you want this job?" question. When they ask why do you want this job, they're asking about the specific position and why it appeals to you and what you're hoping to achieve in it. When they ask you why you want to work for them, they're asking you what you know about their company and what appeals to you about them. Although your first thought might be, "The salary!" Don't lead with that. In fact, I wouldn't even mention that. This is your chance (again) to show what you know about the company. You can balance that with what you're looking for in a company. A mistake people make here is by only talking about what they want to get out of the job. They should spin it so that the first few things they say are actually more what the company can get out of it. Anytime you're selling anything, you should always lead with how this will benefit the other person and then follow up with how it will benefit you. But so many people make the mistake of just leading right in with what they, themselves stand to gain out of something. And remember, a job interview is nothing more than a sales pitch. You're pitching yourself.

Many people would answer the "Why do you want to work here question as follows: "I want to work here because the salary is good and the benefits are good and it seems like a good working environment where I can do what I love and advance my career."

While there's nothing glaringly wrong about that answer, it will not be very impressive to the hiring manager. Your answer should be ordered the following way:

1). Start with what you can do for the company (and spin it like you're giving them reasons why you want to work there)

2). Then talk about what you know about the company and why that makes it attractive to you

3). Finish with how it will help you in your personal goals and what benefits you stand to gain (do not talk about money)

Example:

Why do you want to work here?

I really want to be able to use my skills and experience to contribute real value to an organization. I have a lot to bring to the table and I really want to be with a company that can make use of my skills and talents. I am passionate about helping companies grow and love to be in a position where I can serve and contribute to the health of the overall organization.

Furthermore, ABC Company is so inspiring to me because of the emphasis they place on individuality. It seems like a place where they really encourage diverse thought and ideas. From what I know about ABC company, they give everyone a chance to be part of their growth and they encourage everyone to develop professionally as the company develops. I also really like that one of the company's core values is open-mindedness. This basically supports what I was just saying about the company supporting individual ideas and diversity. I'm also really inspired by CEO Jerry Jones and his amazing story.

Lastly, I think this is a great place for me to advance in my career. I can tell that there will be real challenges I'll face here that will help me grow and develop as a professional. I am very attracted to the open and caring company culture and I feel like it's a great environment for personal as well as professional growth.

This example is fairly generic simply because we're trying to demonstrate a framework for how you can answer this question. You'll want to make your answers a bit more targeted, concise. Think about how you would change this response to reflect what's true about you and the company you're interviewing with. With this type of answer, you're showing them that you have their best interest at heart, you know and respect the company, and that you also see real value in working for them which could make you a happy and eager employee (what every employer wants).

- **Where do you see yourself in 5 years?**

   Most people butcher this question. While a poor answer to this question probably won't take you out of the running, you'll want to understand the question and answer it properly. There's a hidden motive behind this question. Often the hiring manager is trying to find out if you're planning on leaving the company after a few years. They're looking to see if you want to make a career with them or if you simply see them as a stepping stone to a better job somewhere else. Regardless of how you feel about this question, you should always make it sound like you want a career with the company and that you're here to stay. Employers are not naïve. They know that employees come and go based on life changes and career interest, but they want someone with the right attitude. They want someone that sees real value in the company and wants to stay for as long as they can and advance within the company. It is very expensive and time consuming to hire and train a new person so companies do not want to hire someone that's just going to jump ship a year or two down the road. The SHRM study found that on average, it costs an employer 6-9 months of an employee's salary to hire and train a new person. This could mean that in your first year, a company will hardly get any ROI from hiring you. In light of that fact, its more understandable why companies are so discerning and careful when it comes to their hiring decisions.

You can give a generic answer to this question to avoid over-committing, or you can talk about their company specifically and how you hope to grow there. If you're interviewing for a consulting job and hope to become partner or a manager eventually, you can say something like:

In 5 years, I want to be an industry expert in industrial managerial consulting. I know this company is the right environment for me to get there. I want to be able to learn from the best and give back by using my skills to help others learn and by eventually helping to lead the company. I am looking for a career and a livelihood, not just a job.

- **Why do you want to leave your current company?**

     Be careful with this question. This is not an opportunity for you to bad mouth your old company or to speak poorly of your boss or to talk about how you were not treated fairly. It is almost always a bad sign when an employee starts badmouthing his old or current employer. When an employer asks this question, they're usually looking for red flags. They want to know if you're on good terms with your previous or current employer. You can give just a simple generic answer to this question to basically avoid having to go into the details.

     You can say something like: my time at company A was well spent and I learned so much there. I think I was really able bring a lot of value. At this time, they're starting to move in a different direction, away from where my interests lie and It seemed that there really weren't many opportunities left there. That's when I saw this opportunity and it just looked so perfect, that I had to go after it.

- **What makes you unique?**
     This is obviously only something you can answer. It's a tough question and almost aggressive because it's operating on the premise that you are unique and that you will have a good answer to this question. At the end of the day, every one is unique. No two of us are exactly alike, but your uniqueness may or may not be applicable to the job at hand. If there isn't an obvious answer, you can just talk about your experience and skills and how they present a unique skill set. Or else, if you've done something out of the ordinary that provided you a unique perspective, you can talk about that. If all else fails, you can say something

about how you provide a unique perspective, and that your ability to think outside the box and creatively solve problems make you unique. Depending on the feel and vibe of the interview, you can also mention something about personal interests or accomplishments that might make you unique. It's always good to tie these back to your professional skills and make them relevant.

Example: *Well I think I'm a very driven person that will do whatever it takes to achieve a goal or objective. When I was 25 I decided to train for the Iron Man competition. It was one of the hardest things I've ever done, but it gave me a lot of confidence and made me feel like I can do anything I set my mind to.*

- **What do you know about our company?**
  We've already talked about this question to some extent earlier in the book. You should know a couple of basic facts about the company:
    o You should know who the CEO is.
    o You should be able to remember a few of the company's core values and at least read over the mission statement.
    o Know how long the company has been in operation
    o Know roughly how large the company is (either in terms of revenue, or number of employees or both)

  You should demonstrate a basic understanding of what the company does, and which markets it operates in. You should also know a bit about the history of the company and if the company has been bought and sold and who owns it now. If possible, you should know who their main customers are.

You should also understand how the company positions itself. Read headlines, see if the company has been in the news recently. Check the company's website and try to get a feel for what their brand is all about. How are they positioning themselves? What do they claim as their competitive edge? What do they claim to be the best at?

Jot down a few bullet points on this and try to hit them in your answer. The hiring manager is not expecting you to be an expert on their company or know everything there is to know, they just want to see if you've done some homework. It's also interesting for them to see how an outsider perceives their company.

- **How did you prepare for today's interview?**

This will be an honest answer and a synthesis of a lot of what we've already covered in this book. This is actually a very common question. You want to be prepared with a good answer. You can mention that you read this book if you want, but at least discuss what you did to study up on the company. You may have led press releases, studied the company's social media presence (especially Twitter and LinkedIn). You may have carefully studied the company's website, browsed news headlines about the company. Talk about any type of research you did on the company. This can include employee satisfaction-type research. However, it's worth noting, if you didn't find a lot of positive feeback about the company, it'd be best not to bring up the employee satisfaction piece at all. In fact, if all you can find online are comments from disgruntled employees, you should see that as a red flag. Websites like Glassdoor.com do a great job of providing employee-driven information about the company. This website works particularly well for large companies because they have more data to work with.

Glassdoor can give you information on:
- Employee satisfaction with the company: the company will have an overall rating which is based on reviews and ratings by employees
- CEO Approval rating: you can see how well people approve of the CEO and you can read comments about company leadership
- Salary and Benefits: you can get some intel on what people in different positions at the company are making as an average salary. You can often also read comments about the quality of benefits offered, PTO etc.
- Interview Tips and questions: people will often post questions they were asked in interviews. This can be helpful to scan through what people have written and make sure you're prepared for any curveballs that could come your way.

Note: only discuss positive things you read on Glassdoor. For example: "I was so impressed to see your 4-star rating on Glassdoor. I saw so many positive employee comments. If employees were motivated enough to leave a positive review, that speaks very highly of the company and the way they treat their employees." Or you could say something like, "I think it's really awesome that your CEO has such a high approval rating. It's so important in companies of this size, that people feel they are being led by a strong figure that has his employees' best interest at heart." Or if you wanted to say something about the benefits, just keep it general. "I noticed on Glassdoor that people were particularly positive about the benefits the company offers. I think the 401K match is a great investment in your employees. It seems like you're really trying to make this a great place to work and your employees see that."

Note: don't bring up salary information you may have seen on Glassdoor in the interview. You can use it as a bargaining chip later, and you can use it as a basis for your salary expectations. Just keep it general. In your negotiations later when the company makes you an offer, you can just say, "I know the typical salary for this role is, "X."

Answering the, "How did you prepare for today's interview," should not be difficult since you're following the advice of this book and doing as much prep and research beforehand as possible. You'll want to reference multiple sources here:

- Company website
- News media
- Financial reporting (if applicable)
- Glassdoor
- Social media

Make sure you have also done some industry research as well. As we mentioned earlier, you should try to have at least a basic understanding of where the company is positioned in the industry, what their competitive advantage is, and who the other main players are. Using websites like, Hoovers and ThomasNet as well as all of the free public information offered by the US Census Bureau is a great place to find industry info.

- **Why do you want this job?**

  As mentioned above, this is a different question than, "Why do you want to work for us?" Here is where you can talk about your skills, industry knowledge, and how this job is a supposed "perfect fit" for you. You can really hammer home the value that you bring to the table and how this is a perfect advancement in your professional career for you. Even though they're asking you about the job specifically and not the company, you should still start by expressing how excited and enthusiastic you are about the company and the opportunity. You should go after any chance you have to share what you know about the company, job or industry. Since you probably won't be asked all the questions listed here, you'll want to use every opportunity where you can "show off" what you know and how your skills align with what they're looking for.

  You don't want to go overboard on every question because it will show the interviewer that you don't know how to shut up or you don't know how to be concise. If you've already done a fair amount of talking, you can just keep this answer short and simple.

  1. Start with talking about the company and how the fact that the position is with their company is the

biggest reason you want this job. (This will show them that you don't just want any job in the industry. This will show them that you are invested in and sincerely interested in their company and their unique approach to the industry.)

2. Next briefly touch upon the reasons why you are perfectly suited for this job. Don't go overboard here because you will have plenty of other opportunities to talk about your skills and qualifications. You can say it as simply as, "Also, when I read the job requirements and did some more research on your company and the position, it seemed like this position would be absolutely perfect for my skillset, experience and interests. It really seemed like the perfect job for me."

3. Lastly, tie it into your career goals and your desire for professional and personal growth. Make it sound like this is a permanent step for you (even if it's not). You don't want them to get the impression that you're just using this job as a stepping stone to get somewhere better (even if you are).

Overall, just make sure your answer shows that you're excited about the company specifically, you're a perfect fit for the job, and that the job makes sense for you professionally.

- **Tell me about yourself**

This is one of the hardest questions people face in interviews. No one ever knows how to answer this question and very few people answer it well. Often, this is the first question in an interview and not only does it set the tone for the rest of the interview, but it might make the interviewer see you as a strong or weak candidate depending on your response.

Before we talk about how you should answer this question, we'll talk about what most people do and why you should not do that.

Most people answer this question in one of two ways, or a combination of both.

1. They either answer the question by launching into a long-winded life-story. They talk about personal matters, (their family, hobbies etc.) and they just basically walk the interviewer through their life to date.

2. They basically just recapitulate their resume. They just recite what's on their resume without really answering the question.

The problem with these answers is that they make you sound like a weak candidate. The interviewer is looking for a concise, targeted answer to their question that is based only on what's relevant to the interview. It's fine to share personal details sprinkled throughout the interview. You can mention something about your family or hobbies, but don't lead with this as your first answer to the first question. This is where you're going to make your first impression, so this is your biggest and best chance to give your 30 second elevator pitch. Kathryn Minshew, CEO and Founder of The Muse, talks about the Present, Past and Future strategy for answering this question.

Start with what you're currently doing (for example

what you're doing in the current job you're leaving), then talk about what you did before that, and finish with what you're hoping to do (what you're hoping to accomplish with the company you're interviewing with.)

This can be a great approach for answering the "Tell me about yourself," question because it cuts right to the chase. You're choosing to answer with your most compelling skills and experience that will tell the interviewer why they should hire you.

Here's an example: Let's say you have experience in sales and you're interviewing for a management job:

"I'm currently a top-performing account manager for ABC Company where I manage all the new and recurring business in a geographical territory of 5 states. Before that I worked for a Fortune 20 Health Group where I managed key accounts and was tasked with the responsibility of keeping our highest performing accounts happy as well as leading and training all of the Territory Managers. The industry knowledge and managerial expertise I gained in those roles made me realize how excited I am to share that knowledge and expertise with others and manage a team of people instead of accounts. That's what brings me before you today."

If the "Present, Past, Future," method doesn't work for you, you can follow a more general format. Talk first very specifically about your relevant skills and experience, then talk about your most relevant strengths and abilities. Each part should only be a few seconds. Your total answer should take less than 1 minute.

Another example: *"As a top-performing Territory Manager for ABC company with 7 years of industry experience under my belt, I know what it takes to drive performance in this industry. I've been tasked with taking on new territories, reviving declining territories, as well as growing and expanding existing territories. I've proven time and again that I know how to exceed aggressive sales targets, and as a Senior Territory manager, I was our departmental leader in sales and was tasked with on-the-ground training of all new Territory Managers.*

What made me such a great salesman is what will make me an even better manager. I know how to motivate people, lead people, excite people, and I can overcome any challenge. Managing a diverse client base helped me develop a nuanced management style that meets the person or prospect where they're at where I then help them achieve their specific goals and overcome their specific obstacles. As passionate as I am about sales, I'm even more passionate about managing a sales team which is why I'm so excited about this opportunity at XYZ company."

This question cuts right to the heart of what they're looking for. If you're applying to be a sales manager, they want to know, if you have sales experience, how your experience is relevant to management, and if your skills and strengths are relevant to sales management. Of course you will have other forms of experience and many other skills and strengths that you could talk about, but you want to talk only about what you think will be most important to them in a prospective candidate.

- **How did you hear about this position?**

This is a simple question and a simple response is fine. Yet many people still manage to mess this question up. People often use this question as a way to ramble on again about things they've already talked about or about what they'll have an opportunity to talk about later. Also, people sometimes forget where they heard about a job because they've been applying to so many jobs. If you can't remember where you heard about the job, it's not necessarily a big deal, but it may show the interviewer that you've been applying to a lot of jobs and may make your claims that "this is the perfect one and only job for you" less credible.

If you have nothing notable or remarkable to say to this question, just answer it simply, and make sure you remember beforehand, where you heard about the job. If you heard about it from a friend, colleague or current employee of the company or employer, this is a great opportunity for you to mention them. You can say something brief about, *"My friend Tarah told me about this opportunity. She's the Billing Supervisor here and she's had nothing but great things to say about this company. I guess that must be why she's been here for 10 years."*

That's all you have to say. You're subtly name dropping and paying the company a compliment without overdoing it.

- **What type of work environment do you prefer?**
  As with nearly every question you're asked, you'll want to custom tailor your answer so that it aligns with the company you're interviewing with. Even if your ideal working environment would be working from home in your underwear, you'll want to give an answer that

describes the working environment of the company you're interviewing with. This will require some research on your part. It always helps if you can talk to someone that works there. Reading comments on Glassdoor and other employment websites can help give you some insight. Showing up early and observing what you can while you're waiting can give you a nice sneak peak of the working environment as well.

Logistical Questions:

- **Are you willing to relocate?**
  Honesty is the best policy here. A simple yes or no answer is usually the right answer, but if you're unsure, you can always say, "yes," and then plan to negotiate if they make you an offer. However, if you say yes, then they make you an offer and you decide that you're unwilling to relocate, not only is there a possibility that they'll retract their offer, but you may make them angry and disgruntled for misleading them in the interview.

- **Are you willing to travel?**
  As long as you're willing to do at least a little bit of traveling, you should answer "yes" to this question. Discerning and evaluation the level of travel required can come later in the process if you're willing to move forward. Alternatively, if you like to travel or if you're looking for a job where you travel, you can turn this into an opportunity to express your desire to travel as a strength. You can say something like, *"I'm the kind of person*

that does best when I'm in front of the customer face-to-face, so I'm more than willing to travel. Any way that I can interact directly with my customers to drive sales and improve customer relations is a win for me."

- **Would you work holidays and weekends?**
  This is a question you'll have to evaluate for yourself. If this is the type of job where you may be required to come in on holidays and weekends, you'll have to consider if you want the job badly enough. Generally speaking, the only acceptable answer to this question is yes. You can always negotiate further down the road in the process. Often this question is merely to measure your level of dedication. You may not actually ever be required to work holidays and weekends, they just want to make sure that you would be devoted to your work and willing to go the extra mile when required.

- **What's your availability?**
  If this is a full-time job where you'd be working normal business hours, this question may be irrelevant. But if it's a part-time job or hourly/non-traditional job, you'll want to make sure your availability aligns with their business needs. If you're unsure of the answer they're looking for, you can just say, "my availability is flexible and I can make myself available for whatever's needed." If you have other responsibilities, other jobs, or restricted availability, make this clear. You do not want to deceive the interviewer into thinking you can work certain hours if you're unable to do so.

- **When can you start?**

  Typically, this is not a job offer. When they're asking when you can start, they're trying to understand when they'd be able to bring you on board if they decided to hire you. There are also red flags the interviewer is looking for here. If you're currently employed and you tell them that you can start immediately, the interviewer may be unimpressed with the way you're leaving your current employer. If applicable, you should express that you're going to do your duty to your current employer. For example you could say that you'd have to give your two weeks and could start any time after that. This shows the interviewer that you are a competent and respectful employee. The way you treat your current employer speaks volumes about how you will treat your prospective and future employers, so always keep that in mind when answering these questions.

Situational questions:

NOTE: *Situational questions are often the questions people dread the most in Job interviews. It's hard to think of examples under pressure, and people often get flustered or thrown for a loop. That's why its best to brainstorm ideas and answers ahead of time so you're more prepared and don't have to come up with a story on the spot.*

- **Tell me about a time when you made a professional mistake**

  You'll want to answer this question with a valid mistake you made, but then how you fixed the problem. You shouldn't choose a huge mistake, but something that happened and how you resolved it. They're looking more for, "how did you resolve this problem?" Than, "what was the problem." They're also looking for any red flags. If you take the question too seriously and tell them about some inexcusable problem you caused, or make it sound like you have a history of making mistakes, they will not be impressed. Keep it simple and talk about how you resolved the mistake. For example:

I got my dates mixed up and accidentally double-booked client meetings on the same day in two different states. I didn't realize my mistake until it was too late to reschedule, but luckily, I had built up so much rapport and had a really good relationship with the one client, that they were very understanding and happy to reschedule at the last minute.
Since then, I've kept all my appointments carefully organized on my calendar so I ensure that never happens again.

- **Tell me about a time when you faced conflict in the workplace?**

Much like the last question, they are looking to hear how you resolved or handled the conflict. They want to make sure you're not going to be a person that causes unnecessary conflict or someone who can't handle conflict. Conflict is inevitable in most work environments. If your role is going to be client facing, you can talk about a time you faced conflict with a client. If your role is internal facing, you could talk about a situation where you had a conflict with coworkers.

Here's an example: *In my role with ABC company, we had a client who was consistently dissatisfied with every project. Each time we submitted a completed project, the client always complained and demanded revision. It was difficult because their complaints were always unpredictable and it felt like they were simply determined to find fault with every project. I started having weekly phone calls with the client to discuss the ongoing projects. We also started putting together mid-term webinars to show them our progress to date. This made the client feel much more involved in the process and they were able to better direct the project and as a result, they were satisfied with all projects moving forward. It was a great learning experience for our company and it was a practice we started offering for any client that wanted it. It's really helped increase our value in the market.*

- **Tell me about a time when you disagreed with your boss about something.**

    This one is tough because the situation is delicate and you don't want to make them think you're a person who goes over people's heads or who challenges authority. Keep your answer simple and use an example that had a positive resolution. What they're really looking for here is an ability to communicate professionally.

For example: *We had a departmental meeting and our boss told us all that due to budget restraints, the company was restricting travel. After the meaning, many of the sales people were very angry. They were afraid they were going to lose clients or else not be able to win clients without being able to meet them in person. Many of them were complaining to each other. I thought it'd be better to bring the concern up to my boss directly instead of complaining with everyone else. In private, I expressed my concern about how this would affect my client relationships. He thanked me for bringing this to my attention, and told me the restriction was only temporary and it was only set to last to the end of that fiscal year (2 more months).*

- **Tell me about a time when you were asked to do something that wasn't part of your job description?**

You want to express that you're a team player and willing to roll with the punches here. If you come across as inflexible or unwilling to do anything that's not expressly stated in your job description, that will be an issue for your interviewer.

Here's an example of a good response: *We had a territory manager leave the company and so her territory was vacant for a few months while they looked for the right person to take over the territory. My boss asked me to help maintain the territory in addition to my existing responsibilities. I was happy to do it and got to know the new territory pretty well. When they did hire someone, my boss asked me to train the new employee since I had knowledge of the territory. I was really happy to be able to contribute, and I always enjoy helping other people.*

- **Tell me about a time you exercised leadership?**

Regardless of what type of position you held in the past, there is surely a time where you exercised some form of leadership. It could be something very basic or something very significant. You'll want to show a situation where you stepped up to the plate or where you led your coworkers. If you had a position where you had people reporting to you, this would be very easy. Otherwise, just pick a time where you took charge of something or stood out in some way.

Example: *My boss was out for a few days and we got a massive order from a new client with no information on how to process the order. Normally, our supervisor handled new client relationships and orders of that size, but I asked my coworkers to pitch in, and we all worked hard to get the order placed right away. Our timely response impressed the new customer and helped solidify our relationship with them.*

- **Tell me about the last time a customer or coworker got angry with you:**
Similar to the, "Dealing with a difficult customer or employee question," the interviewer is looking to see how you handle that sort of pressure and interpersonal conflict. Do not make the mistake of acting like such things never happen to you. Some people think it will make them look better if they act as though they get along with everyone and have never had a workplace conflict. This is not the answer they're looking for, and 90% of the time they won't buy it anyway. Give an example of a situation where a customer or coworker got angry with you and how you alleviated their anger, solved the problem and forged ahead stronger than ever.

- **How do you deal with pressure and deadlines in the workplace?**
Usually the best answer to this question is to make it sound like you thrive off of pressure and deadlines. This will depend on the job in question and as always, you should try to be as honest as possible. You can indirectly

79

answer the question by saying that you're experienced with pressure in the workplace and that you always meet deadlines. For example you could say, *"In my role with ABC company, I faced a lot of tight deadlines and a lot of pressure from upper management as the sales department head. We were often given very tight deadlines with very little notice, so I got used to working that way and taking it all in stride. I'm more than capable of handing high-pressure situations and deadlines."*

Or if you want to make an even stronger impression, you could say something like: *"I thrive in high-pressure, high-stakes environments. When I was a territory manager for X Company, I actually started in a role that was 100% commission. That's a lot of pressure because if I didn't make sales, I didn't make anything. However, I became one of the top salesmen and made money than many of my colleagues who were in salaried jobs. I thrive off of pressure and I always meet deadlines usually operating ahead of schedule."*

- **Off the wall company culture questions and brain teasers:**

  These days as companies and workplaces are becoming more and more non-traditional, employers are more and more commonly using strange off-the-wall interview questions or else posing some kind of brain teaser or riddle as part of the interview. These kinds of questions often completely throw people for a loop. They are usually unprepared for them and don't know how to answer. They typically end up stuttering, blanking out, or shooting from the hip and saying something awkward or inappropriate.

While the motivations for asking these questions may vary, often the employer is looking to see how you respond to pressure and how you handle curve balls. In the prospective job, you may well encounter off-the-wall situations or clients and the employer wants to see if you can take it in stride and think on your feet or if you just cave when confronted with something unexpected. That said, don't put too much pressure on yourself here because the question, *"If you could be any animal, what animal would you be?" likely won't be the most important question you answer in the interview.*

There are a few things you can plan to do to make a good impression here. While you won't necessarily be able to plan an answer to these questions because they are usually random and surprising, you can at least control your demeanor and the way you answer the question.

A good way to buy time when someone asks you an unexpected question is to smile (or laugh) if appropriate and say something like, "Wow! That's a great question." And then you can say something like, "Let me think about that, I've never been asked that before." This is a genuine and honest response. If you just rapidly fire off an answer, it will make the interviewer think everything you say is scripted or else, you haven't really put thought into your answer.

If you can't think of a good job-related answer to the question, then pick an answer that is either funny, or at the very least won't be seen as negative. For example, if you're asked, what type of animal would you be, don't answer: "A sloth because I'm lazy and just like to do nothing all day." That would be one of the worse possible answers. If you're interviewing for a sales job, you could say, "A lion, because I'm always on the hunt for great deals and new business." This answer sounds a little bit disingenuous (like you're just telling them what they want to hear), but it isn't a bad answer nonetheless. If you can think of a unique and genuine answer on the spot, that would be the best approach. For example: "I think I'm a greyhound. I'm the kind of person that can wear people down with perseverance. When I decide to do something or go after something, I see it all the way through to the very end. Even though the cheetah might be faster than me in the beginning, I always outdistance him in the end because I pace myself and persevere and keep my eyes on the prize."

After answering, it can be a good tactic to follow up with a question like, "Did that answer the question?" Or you could say something like, "What an interesting question. What have other people said?" or if you're feeling bold, "How would you answer that question?"

For some technical jobs especially in engineering and math-related fields, you may be asked to solve a riddle or a brain teaser. The goal here isn't necessarily to get the right answer (although that would be great), but it's to show the interviewer that you understand what's being asked of you and you can answer the question in a systematic logical way. You'll want to try to give a reasonable, defensible answer. You'll want to be able to show them how you arrived at that answer and what system and steps you followed to get that answer. In these types of professions, precision and systems are key. You don't just want to take a wild guess, you want to show that you can take steps to give a reasonable answer to the question. A way to demonstrate a method is by asking qualifying questions. For example, you might be asked something like, "How many tennis balls can you fit in a 747?" You could follow up with questions like, "Can I fill the overhead compartments?" Although this may not be a mind-blowing question, it shows that you can think critically and ask the right questions. These are qualities prospective employers are looking for in candidates.

The Tough Questions:

- **Why were you fired?**
  Unlike many other questions where you really want to dig in and put as much into your answer as possible, you want to keep this answer short, pointed and try to change to another subject as soon as possible without being evasive.

If the firing happened several years ago and you've had another job since then, it will be fairly easy to answer. You can say something like, *"At the time there was some miscommunication between my boss and I. I didn't fully understand what was being asked of me, and he didn't fully understand how to communicate. It was a new company and so it was new territory for a lot of us. The opportunity provided me a lot of learning experiences and lessons for growth and as you can see I went on to be quite successful with company ABC."*

If this firing happened recently, you can brush it off by saying something like,
"In retrospect, I'm kind of glad it happened because it really pushed me to pursue other opportunities in areas where I really excel and feel passion and interest."

Or you can keep it vague and generic, *"Unfortunately things just weren't working out, but I'm still grateful for the experience and learned a lot from it."*

There are many ways you can answer it, but you want to avoid saying something that is going to take you out of the running for the job. On the one hand, you don't want to completely evade the question, but you don't want to be overly direct if there was a serious problem that caused you to be fired from your last job.

Keep in mind that if you lie in the interview, you will almost surely not be offered the job. Even worse, if you lie in the interview, they hire you, and then later find out that you lied in your interview, that's grounds for immediate termination. They can easily check with your previous employer and get their side of the story, so be careful not to say anything that can be misconstrued as dishonest or aggressive. Be humble and make it sound like it was a learning experience for you and that you're not worried about it moving forward because it was a one-time issue.

- **Why were you laid off?**

  This question is easier to answer because it may well not have been your fault. There could be many reasons why someone would be laid off and you don't need to worry about it too much about having this on your employment record as long as you can spin it so the layoff does not sound like it was based on your merit or value to the company.

  Most often, companies implement layoffs when they're not doing well financially. If you were one of several or many people laid off, you can just say, *"Unfortunately, the company was going through some financial upheaval. We lost several of our biggest clients due to new governmental regulation. As a result, they had to lay off 10% of their workforce and I was included in that portion."*

  There could be other reasons why you might be laid off. For example, new VP's and Executive leadership, and they come in and appoint new directors and upper level management. This is quite common. Or else, the company is experiencing an organizational change and they're getting rid of certain departments or changing direction and laying off some people and bringing on others. Whatever the reason is, you just need to spin it so that it sounds like the layoff was due to circumstances beyond your control. Make it clear that it did not reflect your value in the company and that it was due to larger company-wide initiatives or industry dynamics.

- **Why was there an unemployment gap?**

This is not necessarily something that will count significantly against you—especially if you're able to give a good answer. They'll want to know what motivated you to leave the workforce, and what you did while you were gone and what made you come back. If you were gone for several years, or if there are multiple significant gaps, you will have more explaining to do. You'll also want to make it clear that you're back in the workforce to stay this time (even if you're not sure about that). You want to alleviate the concern that you will leave the company on another employment gap in the near future.

If you can talk about some personal or professional value you gained during your employment gap, especially if its applicable to the job at hand, that will be a way of actually turning it into a strength—not a weakness.

For example: *I took some time off to devote my full attention to getting my MBA. I know that I could have continued to work during that time, but I'm of the belief that it's better to do one thing well instead of doing several things mediocrely. As such, I was able to put my nose to the grindstone and graduated top of my class with my MBA.*

If you took a gap for personal or family reasons, it's fine to give a very brief, honest explanation, and make it clear that it was a one-time situation in the past and you don't anticipate it being an issue in the future.

For example: *I took a year off to take care of my aunt who had been diagnosed with a debilitating disease. She's been able to get in-*

home care now which has made everything much more manageable for her and allowed me to return to work.

- **What other companies are you interviewing with?**

You don't want to answer this question by saying, "You're the only company I'm interviewing with." That gives all the negotiating power to them and you want to avoid that. You will want to make it sound like you have other options, but this one is the most appealing to you. You can say something as simple as: *"I have a number of opportunities I'm pursuing in the industry, but this is the one I'm most excited about."* Or, you can be much more specific if you so choose. You can say, *"I'm interviewing with ABC Company and DEF Company for Senior Category Management roles, but I have to tell you that based on what I've learned about this position and your company, I feel like this is the perfect fit for me."*

- **What is your greatest professional achievement?**

Pam Skillings of "Big Interview" recommends taking the STAR approach which is a common approach to discussing a problem or situation. STAR is an acronym for the process: Situation, Task, Approach, Response.

This is basically where you take what might be one of your greatest professional achievements, and start with the preliminary situation. Tell them what the current state was before you started the initiative, what the task at hand was, how you approached the situation and what the response to your approach/solution was.

Not everyone is able to say they came up with some revolutionary strategy that saved the company millions of dollars or else they landed a huge client that no one else was able to woo. Sometimes you may feel like you don't have a lot of big accomplishments to show yet. The important thing is to have a few examples—even if they seem insignificant to you. It's all about how you pitch them. This is not a time to be humble—it's not a time to downplay your experience. It's a time to brag. Make it sound as significant and important as you can.

Example: *"One of the most exciting and notable achievements in my time with ABC company was when we launched a new product category. As a category manager, I was pulled away from the products I knew to work on a special task force to build this new category from the bottom up. It was extremely challenging but very rewarding.*

My approach was multi-faceted. The first few months of the project consisted of collecting a huge amount of market data and analyzing the data. I was able to build a database where we were able to easily manipulate the data and look at trends that helped us in our rollout. Our market testing phase was even more intensive but we were meticulous with our attention to detail. Therefore, at the final rollout, we had almost no hiccups. It was one of the company's most successful category rollouts and we were able to capture 10% market share in the first year. Our team was awarded special recognition by the company leadership. It was a really incredible experience."

Let's say you don't have anything that significant to share. Maybe you were a customer service representative in your past job and didn't have as much opportunity for giant accomplishments. Here's a simpler example that could work:

As a customer service representative, there's a delicate balance between customer satisfaction and efficiency. Although our supervisors wanted us to treat each customer with complete respect and courtesy, they also wanted us to get through a significant number of phone calls in a day. Many representatives found it difficult to find the balance. Either they'd spend too long on the phone with customers in an attempt to make them happy, or else they'd start getting lower customer satisfaction ratings because they were rushing customers off the phone to do get through more calls.

I brought this to the attention of my manager, and we had some ongoing discussions and departmental meetings about it. We were able to start a new incentive program with the customer service and billing departments. The new incentive proportionately weighted call numbers and customer satisfaction numbers. This incentivized people to find the right balance of service and efficiency with their calls.

From the reporting we received, it looked like the incentive was working because customer satisfaction was rising as were the call numbers. It felt really good to be able to suggest a change that not only helped me and my coworkers, but really helped the company as well.

- **What's your dream job?**

  You may or may not get this question, but it's a chance for you to plug (once again) your commitment to your career and hopefully, the company that's interviewing you. You can start with something light-hearted like, *"My dream when I was a kid was to be an astronaut. But once I found out how bad the food was, I changed my mind."* This is a funny response that kind of disarms the question. After you say something like that, then you can give a practical and real answer that doesn't sound like you're just telling them what they want to hear.

  Usually it's better to give a general description of what your ideal job looks like instead of giving a specific job title. Try to think of a job description that's actually attainable within the company that you're interviewing with. It could be a job that's quite a few steps above the one you're interviewing for, but that just shows that you're ambitious and thinking about the future. As long as your answer doesn't cause them to be concerned that you're going to leave them after a short time or that you're using this job as a stepping stone to a better job, you will be fine.

- **How would your boss and your coworkers describe you?**

Don't be too humble here, but don't be over the top either. You can qualify your answers with "I think," or, "I'd imagine." To make it sound less canned. This is another opportunity for you to really focus on the skills the interviewer is looking for the most. Let's say that you're interviewing for a finance role and you perceive that the interviewer values independence and autonomy. You could say something like, *"I think my boss would say that I'm one of his most reliable employees who has excellent eye for detail, always meets deadlines, and can solve complex financial problems with minimal guidance."*

About your coworkers, you could say, *"They'd describe me as a team player who is always ready to pitch in. Many of my coworkers regularly come to me with questions about work."*

- **What would your first 30, 60, 90 days look like in this role?**

This is a very difficult question for most people because you probably don't yet know specifically what you will be doing. You don't know what their expectations will be. Generally, you'll want to follow these guidelines:
   o First 30 days: Undergo training, get acquainted with all my coworkers and supervisors and start to understand my job responsibilities
   o First 60 Days: Getting up to speed on the current state of projects I'll be working on, getting into a workflow. Understanding the current cadence of work. Understanding company goals and strategies.
   o First 90 Days: Ongoing learning and training, but starting to develop my own approach. Developing

a workflow for myself, and starting to set goals and objectives for my work.

You can make these points more specific based on the job responsibilities, but keeping it general and to the point is fine. They just want to see how well you can formulate ideas on the spot. They will definitely have more direction for you if they hire you.

- **How would you fire someone?**

This question is common especially if you're interviewing for a managerial role or any role where you will have people reporting to you. The most important points here are to make sure you come across like you'd be comfortable with this situation. You don't want to appear timid or like you wouldn't be able to handle the situation. Make sure you emphasize that you'd closely adhere to company protocol and you'd be firm but respectful.

You could say something like, *"I'd start by familiarizing myself with company protocol on employee termination if this was new territory for me, and consult with the HR department. Then I'd schedule a meeting with the employee and respectfully notify the employee (in person if possible) of their termination and explain the reasons why they're being terminated. I'd answer any questions they may have and be sure to document everything appropriately."*

A simple, straightforward answer is what they're looking for. You're showing your competent and would be able to efficiently and effectively handle sensitive employee situations.

- **What do you like to do outside of work?**

    This is a typical question you may or may not hear. While it's certainly not the most important question you'll be asked in your interview, it is an opportunity for you to make yourself stand out or to create a memorable moment that will stand out in the mind of the interviewer when he is later reflecting on the various applicants and interviews. Try to avoid boring or generic responses that everyone probably says. For example, don't say: I like to travel, or, I like to be active, or, I like to spend time with my family. While all of these may be true, they are not interesting. If there's something particularly interesting about your interest in travel, fitness, or your family, share that with them. For example, you can say, *"I have the travel bug! I plan to visit every country in my lifetime, and when I travel, I always try to immerse myself in the food culture. I like to try all the weird adventurous foods and eat where the locals eat and eat it the way they eat it. It's so much fun! Then when I come home, I try to recreate what I tried abroad and force my family to be my guinea pigs."*

Or, *"Any way that I can be active AND be outside is a win for me. My husband and I joined an adult rowing team which is a lot of fun and great exercise. We love getting out on the Bay and rowing early in the morning when the sun is rising and the birds are active. It's the highlight of our day usually."*

Or, *"I invest a lot of my free time in my kids. We like to do a lot of wood working and art projects together. Anything from making seasonal placemats, to building bird houses and picture frames together. We have a work shop in our basement that we like to use as much as possible."*

While none of these responses will make you the world's most interesting person, they're more colorful adaptions of otherwise boring responses. It shows the interviewer you're a well-rounded, real person. That's the goal here.

- **What are your salary expectations?**

     This is a tricky question. You should skirt the question if possible—especially in the initial interview. Do some research on what the company pays for this position and look at what the industry standard for the role is in your area. Glass Door offers a lot of insight into this. You'll also find info on Payscale.com, Salary.com and even the job search engine: Indeed.com. If you can't avoid the question or skirt it with a vague answer, give a range that is in line with your experience and the industry standard that you've researched. If they ask you what you're currently making at your job, you should try to be honest. Generally, it's good to say a number that's 10-20% lower than what you're hoping to be offered in this new role (of course there are exceptions to this role.) To answer this question, you could say: "My salary expectations are consistent with my qualifications and industry trends." Or you could just try to say that you're flexible by saying something like, "If we decide that I'm the best fit for this job, I'm sure we can come to a mutually beneficial agreement on salary."

     You want to avoid sounding like you are only in it for the money, and you also want to avoid sounding inflexible. That said, you also want to avoid selling yourself short and asking for less than you're entitled to.

Companies will usually try to pay you as little as they can get away with, so if they sense that you're willing to take a lower salary, they'll try to convince you that that's the best offer they can give. Conversely, if you aim too high, the company will either feel like you're asking for more than you're worth, or quite simply, they'll worry they won't be able to afford to hire you. So, in conclusion, try to avoid a direct answer to the question, or else provide a fairly wide range to demonstrate your flexibility and avoid under or overpricing yourself.

Part 3: Interviewing

Dressing for Success:

Dress in a manner that is consistent with the job you're trying to score. If you're interviewing for a waiter job, you don't necessarily need to wear a tuxedo, but if you're interviewing for a Marketing Manager job, you don't want to show up in jeans and a T-Shirt either. It's always better to be a bit over-dressed than under-dressed. If you're overdressed, it at least shows the interviewer that you're taking this process seriously and you care about your appearance. If you don't dress well, that will be a huge red flag to the employer. Even if you're perfectly qualified for the job, not dressing appropriately shows that you don't care much about your appearance or even the job in question and that you don't know what it means to act as a professional in the workplace.

For Men: you generally can't go wrong with a suit. If it's not a professional position, a shirt and tie or at the very least a dress shirt and dress pants are recommended.
Invest in a decent suit and a decent shirt and tie with matching belt and shoes. It could be the difference between getting the job and not getting it. The investment will more than pay for itself in the long run. See it as an investment in your career. Typically, a dark suit and a light dress shirt is what is recommended. Depending on the nature of the job, go for a conservative look with a fitted suit that isn't too flamboyant but isn't bulky. When you wear a bulky suit, you tend to look uncomfortable like you

don't usually wear a suit. The resulting image makes you look unprofessional. Shave, comb your hair, make sure your breath is fresh but do not chew gum during the interview. It makes you look careless. Suck a breath mint before going into the interview and then dispose of it or swallow it right before the interview starts. Avoid wearing strongly-scented cologne or deodorant. Try to avoid bright or flamboyant colors.

For women: wear a pantsuit or a suit with a skirt. Go for something flattering, but conservative. Do not take the risk of wearing something edgy or provocative. Choose a dark color and make sure it is tailored to your body and fits you comfortably. Generally a simple, lighter colored shirt or blouse with your suit is the way to go. Err on the side of "less is more." This means don't overdo the accessories, makeup or jewelry. A few modest accessories that compliment your look but are not distracting or flashy are the maximum. As for makeup, keep it simple so that it accentuates your features but is not distracting. Avoid wearing any type of strong perfume. Keep your shoes conservative—this is not the time for stiletto heels. Conservative heels are okay as long as you're able to walk naturally in them. Flats are fine as long as they don't look overly casual. Keep your hair professional and polished and out of your face if possible. Avoid any bright distracting colors or prints or nail polish etc.

Most Common Mistakes People Make in an Interview:

The Problem: Being Hesitant or freezing up.

You may be the kind of person that draws a blank or freezes up when under pressure. Some people are uncomfortable talking about themselves or perhaps uncomfortable talking to people they don't know. Even if you know the answer, sometimes your mind can go blank and you're not sure what to do. You don't want to falter or freeze in the interview. You want to be able to answer decisively and smoothly.

Solution: there are a few things you can do to avoid freezing up:

- **Do your homework:** this is what this book is all about. Preparing for the interview and trying to prep yourself for most of the questions that might be asked of you. If you know your stuff, there's less chance that you'll panic and freeze up.

- **Practicing:** practice saying some of your answers out loud. We mentioned in earlier sections that you want to avoid sounding canned or scripted. You probably won't want to write all your answers out word for word, but jotting down bullet point notes will really help you keep your bearings and hit the main things you want to say in an answer. Practice in front of a mirror and try to assume a confident but humble air.

- **Go on as many interviews as possible:** when you're new to the interview game, the whole idea of an interview can be very daunting and overwhelming. The best way to overcome the fear of interviewing is simply by doing it. Go on as many interviews as possible—even for jobs you think you won't be interested in or jobs you know you're not qualified for. Once you get in the practice of interviewing and you become comfortable with that type of pressure, you'll be able to relax more and be yourself in interviews. Note: this is only really advisable if you're new to interviewing, or if you're rusty and haven't had to interview in a long time. Once you're a seasoned pro, you should only go on interviews that make sense for you.

The Problem: Dominating the Conversation/Talking too Much:

Some people are overly eager to come across as assertive and show that they've done their homework. What ends up happening is that they completely dominate the conversation and rattle off way too much information way too quickly not giving the interviewer opportunity for dialogue or conversation. This can be very off-putting to the interviewer and can also be a red flag when they're considering your ability to do a good job for their company.

The Solution:

o Practicing with friends by doing "mock interviews" where they ask you questions and you try to answer them. Have your friends alert you if you're dominating too much (often other people can see it more readily than we can see it in ourselves)

o Practice being a good listener in conversations with friends.

o Make eye contact and try to read the other person's expression. Usually you can pick up on the other person's non-verbal signals if you're coming on too strong.

o Make a subtle note to yourself in the notes that you
    will bring with you on the interview to "slow down and
    listen." When we are nervous, we often forget to do
    that.

The Problem: Rambling

A pitfall people often fall into is rambling on about something
when they're not quite sure how to answer a question. It can be a
nervous habit, or you can simply be an over-achiever trying to
pack too much into an answer. Although its better to show as
much knowledge as you can, its very easy to go overboard.

The Solution:

o **Answer the question directly** first. Instead of launching
    into a long-winded explanation, give a direct answer first,
    then offer support for that answer afterward.
o **Practice being more concise.** A good way to do this is
    by writing out answers you would give to prospective
    questions and then trying to revise the answers and make
    them shorter without compromising the quality of the
    answer. Often this means cutting out unnecessary fluff
    and getting straight to the meat of whatever you have to
    say
o **Another good idea is to time yourself.** Set a timer for
    30 seconds and try to hit all the points you want to make
    in that time. You can adjust the amount of time you give
    yourself based on the importance and complexity of the
    question. Not only is it good practice and a desirable
    quality in prospective employees to be able to be concise

and to the point, but also, quite frankly, the interviewer doesn't want to listen to you ramble on all day. They want you to answer their questions and then move on.

The Problem: Being too Humble

Many people feel uncomfortable bragging about themselves or making a big deal out of their accomplishments. As a result, they downplay their experience and qualifications. This makes them appear as a weak candidate or else makes the employer feel that they can offer you less money. Both of these are things we want to avoid.

The Solution:

- o Brainstorm a list of your strengths: write down as many as you can think of. Then arrange them in order from most to least relevant/important for the job you're applying for.
- o Think about how you would speak about someone else you respect and want the best for, then try to speak about yourself the same way. For example, if you had a friend that you were recommending for a job, how would you speak about them? You'd focus on their good qualities and talk about why they'd be a good fit without going overboard or making them sound like they were too good to be true.
- o Ask People who love you to help you come up with good responses to, "What are your strengths?" and "Why should we hire you?" and "Why are you the best fit for this job?"

The Problem: Being too confident

Although confidence is key to performing well in an interview, it can quickly turn to cockiness and arrogance which is even less desirable than timidity. Cocky people think they're above the rules or think they don't have to consult with others. They think they know everything and there's nothing new to learn. They also think they're worth a lot of money and will always be looking for higher pay or higher status. These are all undesirable qualities that employers do not want in prospective employees. Most people aren't genuinely cocky or arrogant, they simply make the mistake of coming across that way because they're nervous or overcompensating for their self-consciousness.

The Solution:

- Smile when you speak: it will usually make the interviewer more disposed to like you and give you the benefit of the doubt.
- Speak well of others (example, past bosses/companies, mentors, educators, family members etc.)
- Add some qualifiers like, "I think I am particularly good with…" You can also reference opportunities with qualifiers like, "I was very privileged to be able to experience…" or "it was an incredible opportunity for me and I learned so much." Whenever you can talk about how you learned something, it shows a humility and shows the interviewer that you are open to learning and you know that you don't know everything.

The Problem: Appearing Uninterested

Maybe you're a bit disheartened. Maybe you've been on a lot of job interviews with no success—or maybe pickings are slim and there aren't many opportunities in your area. As a result, you may already feel negative or apathetic when you walk into the interview. The irony is that if you let your interviewer see that, you can almost ensure that you won't get the job. An employer wants a candidate that is not only qualified, but genuinely interested in the company and the opportunity.

The Solution:
- o Smile and engage. Look like you want to be there—even if you don't.
- o Express your excitement and interest. Make the employer feel like your number one goal is to be able to work with their company. Working little phrases into your responses like, "That's why I'm so excited about this opportunity," or, "from everything I know about your company, you really seem to be the absolute best at what you do, and that's something I want to be a part of."
- o Ask engaging questions. If you just ask canned generic questions without apparent desire for a thoughtful answer, you're demonstrating to the interviewer that you don't care that much about the job. In turn, they won't care that much about you as a candidate.

The Problem: Arriving Late for the Interview

There's one nearly sure-fire way to ensure that you don't get the job. That is, being late for the interview. It shows employers that the job opportunity isn't even important enough for you to show up on time. It also shows you lack the professional polish to be able to arrange your affairs so that you're at least on time if not early.

The Solution:

- o No Matter how sure you are of the amount of time it takes to get to the interview location, plan to arrive 20-30 minutes early. Think of this as just giving yourself extra time to prepare and go over your notes.
- o Take into account the time of the interview. Will you run into traffic? Is the interview taking place during peak traffic hours?
- o Make sure you have contact information for the people you're interviewing with. If there's a problem or if you have trouble finding the meeting spot, you'll want to let them know in advance. Nothing is worse than a no-show.
- o Make sure you know all the details of the meeting beforehand. If you're meeting at the office, ask for directions on where to park and how to get into the building and where you should go from there. If you're meeting at a restaurant or public place, make sure to clarify how you will meet. For example: "I'll arrive early and get a table for both of us." Or, "I'll wait in the hotel lobby for you. I'll be wearing a blue suit."

Basically, just try not to leave anything to chance so that you will be sure to be in the right place nice and early without risking missing the interview or being late for it.

The Problem: Oversharing

Many people end up going overboard when they're nervous. This is not the time to talk about your credit card debt or your marital problems. If you overload the interviewer with TMI, you'll appear unstable or at least unprofessional.

The Solution:

o Think before you speak. This is hard when you're under pressure and when you're nervous, but try not to just blurt out whatever pops into your head. Rather, quickly check what you're going to say and ask yourself, "Is this relevant to the job? Is it professional?" if you answer yes, then you can proceed.

o You CAN share random personal tidbits that support your answers or will make the interviewers see you more favorably, but keep these to a minimum. Focus on what's relevant to the job, and avoid "unloading on" your interviewers at all costs.

The Problem: Not Making Eye Contact

In this age of smartphones, people's ability to make eye contact is at an all time low, yet it is important in a job interview. When you fail to make eye contact, you come across as disengaged, awkward and even dishonest. Conversely, when you're able to look the interviewer squarely in the eye, you come across as confident, honest and engaged.

The Solution:

o Practice making eye contact in normal day-to-day conversations with friends and family. You should even practice with random strangers you encounter throughout your day. When you're at the store, make eye contact with the person at the checkout counter and say thank you. When you hold the door for someone make eye contact with them and smile.

o You don't want to stare intensely at them without breaking eye contact either. You want to make eye contact often but not constantly, and when you're not making eye contact, you should try to look as engaged as possible with other non-verbal signals like nodding your head and smiling. In the interview, it's a good idea to take notes, so you can take breaks from making eye-contact to write down notes.

The Problem: Not getting contact info or asking about next steps

You have to keep in mind that you are most likely one of many candidates interviewing for this job. You don't want to make the mistake of passively waiting for the interview to eventually get back to you if they're interested. You want to make it abundantly clear that you're interested in moving forward with the company as soon as possible.

The Solution:

o Ask for the business card of the interviewer at the close of the interview. Many interviewers and managers will give you their card at the start of the interview so this may be an unnecessary step.

o At the close of the interview, reiterate your desire to move forward with the company and ask them what the next steps are. Typically the interviewer will say something generic like, "we have a few more interviews and then we'll be making decisions about second-round interviews." Rarely does the interviewer make any kind of decisive commitment on the spot, but its always a good idea to express your desire to move forward and ask what the next steps are.

The Problem: failing to follow up on the interview

Much like the last point, you are one of many people interviewing for this job. You want to stay in the forefront of the interviewer's mind as long as possible. Failing to follow up tells the interviewer that you don't care about the job or that you're not good at following through.

The Solution: Send a quality follow-up email about 24 hours after the interview. This is a great way to keep the ball rolling and reiterate your interest in the job.

20 Subtle Tips for a Successful Interview (Verbal & Non-Verbal):

1. **Make eye contact**—as mentioned earlier, this is one of the most important ways to establish connection and trust between you and the interviewer. When you make eye contact, you show active interest, competence and confidence. When you fail to make eye-contact, it shows lack of confidence, lack of interest, and lack of trustworthiness.

2. **Firm Handshake**—there's nothing worse than the dead fish handshake in an interview. After the initial greeting, your handshake will be your first connection point between you and the interviewer. Although, it probably won't make or break the interviewer, it's an opportunity to make a strong impression. Having a strong, firm handshake shows that you are confident and ready for the interview. However, out of nervousness, some people are way too firm with their handshakes and try to break the hand of the interviewer. This may be even worse than the dead fish handshake. It can be difficult to gage how the person is going to shake your hand. If you go in for the handshake expecting the other person to give you an equally strong handshake, you may risk crushing their hand if they have a weak handshake. Therefore, Ease into the handshake. Go in with light pressure and apply more pressure as you quickly perceive the level of strength that your interviewer's handshake has.

3. **Smile**—this is not a criminal prosecution. A professional smile shows that you're a pleasant person who is excited about this opportunity and feel reasonably confident about your chances.

4. **Be at Ease**—this one is tough for a lot of people because there are few situations in which they feel less at ease than in a job interview. Relaxing your posture a bit, sitting back in your chair instead of crouching on the edge of your seat, being mindful of any nervous ticks (toe tapping, drumming fingers, shaking limbs etc), eliminating shakiness in your voice—these are all ways to show the interviewer that you're at ease in the proceedings.

5. **Put the interviewer at ease too**—feel the situation out and try to be friendly if appropriate—you can even ask them questions about where they're from etc. This one can leave a very positive impression with the interviewer particularly if the job in question involves any type of customer service or interaction with people. If you have the ability to go into a nerve-racking situation and put everyone in the room at ease, and operate with poise and grace yourself, you will make quite a good impression.

6. **Actively listen.** Make eye contact and show body language that shows you're actively listening to them and you're interested in hearing what they have to say. Incline your head, and lean in ever so slightly. Nod your head whenever the interviewer says something you particularly agree with or identify with.

7. **Be concise**. Practice saying what you want to say, then restating it in fewer words.

8. **Ask more open-ended questions** that will give your insight into the job and be careful not to answer the question for them. Many people make this mistake when they're nervous. They ask a question, then partially answer it for themselves to make their question sound less aggressive. For example: "Why did the previous person in this role leave? Did they find another opportunity somewhere else?" A better way to ask this question is, "Can you tell me anything about why this position became vacant?" You are asking an open-ended question here that opens the door for the interviewer to give you insider information into the company. You may discover something new here that you wouldn't have previously discovered. When you try to answer the question for them, you're giving them an easy way out and minimizing your chances of learning something new. Similarly, you'll want to avoid yes or no questions. For example, "Do you have a way of measuring success for this role?" This is not a good question. A much better way to ask would be, "Can you tell me how success in this role is measured?" It's an open-ended question that seeks to find out as much information as possible.

9. **Make sure you're excited and not cocky.** Temper your bragging with expressions of how excited you are about the opportunity and how much you've learned and how excited you are to continue to learn and develop.

10. Do your best to **come across both positive, and easy-going**. Nobody likes a Debby Downer, but people don't like over positive hyper people either. Seem positive but also down to earth

11. **Don't seem desperate**. Seem at ease—if anything you want to make them feel like they'd be lucky to have you, not the other way around.

12. **Be Careful with Gestures:** Gestures can be great. They can make you seem more lively and animated, but only do what feels (and looks comfortable). Practice with a friend or in front of the mirror. Do not flail wildly and avoid any rapid or alarming motions. If you feel and look awkward while using gestures, keep them minimal.

13. **Appropriate facial expressions.** Be careful not to overthink this. Maintain respectful, engaged facial expressions. Remaining expressionless implies that your mind is blank or else you're not listening to the interviewer. However, if you overdo it with wildly animated facial expressions, you'll come across as bizarre or unstable. It's always good to practice in front of a mirror or with a trusted friend or colleague.

14. **Keep Good Seated Posture:** as stated previously, you want to appear relaxed, but interested and professional. Relax your shoulders in the chair and lean very slightly forward but don't slouch. Keep your lower back pressed against the back of the chair with your feet planted on the

ground. Don't shift your feet around a lot or bounce your legs. Try to remain still but relaxed.

15. **Take Notes.** It's perfectly acceptable and even encouraged to take notes when the interviewer is speaking or answering your questions. Don't overdo it—don't furiously scribble down every word they say, but taking note of something that stands out or seems important to you here and there is perfectly acceptable. This is also a good opportunity for you to narrow down and refine your list of questions for the interviewer. Throughout the interview, some of the questions you've prepared for the interviewer will almost certainly be answered just through conversation. You don't want to ask a question at the end that's already been answered in the course of the interview, so you can cross those questions out as the answers become apparent. However, new questions may occur to you throughout the course of the interview. Jot a quick note to ask them about it when its your turn to ask questions.

16. **Don't interrupt.** When people are nervous, they talk too fast and often don't wait their turn to speak. It's very unattractive when someone is constantly interrupting other people because it implies that they think what they have to say is more important and that they're not interested in listening. Carefully listen to everything the interviewer says and let them finish each thought before beginning your answer or interjecting. If they're in the middle of something that you wanted to address and you're afraid you'll forget to address it when its your turn

to speak, quickly jot a quick note to yourself to reference it when you're answering.

17. **Sell yourself.** This is your chance to take your experience and paint a picture: the interviewer hasn't seen you at your workplace, he doesn't know the mundane specifics of your job. This is your chance to make your role and responsibilities sound as important as possible—even if the day to day was mundane or didn't seem that important.

18. **Arrive at least 15 minutes early**—and look at ease and expectant but not impatient while you're waiting. Review your notes.

19. **Avoid your Phone.** While you're waiting for the interview, don't be glued to your phone. You may just want to leave your phone in the car or at the very least turn it off as soon as you enter the building.

20. After you answer a difficult question, **ask, "Does that answer your question?"** to make sure the interviewer doesn't feel snubbed or like you're trying to avoid a question.

Part 4: Closing the Interview:

Typically, towards the end of the interview, the interviewer will ask you what questions you have for them. This is your chance to use the list you've prepared before the interview. If you've been following the tips in this book, you'll have been carefully refining your questions throughout the interview so that you don't waste the interviewer's time by asking questions that are irrelevant or have already been answered earlier in the interview.

It's perfectly fine to scan your list of questions and say, "Actually a lot of these questions have been answered throughout our interview which is great." This can buy you time while you're searching for the right questions to ask.

Asking Closing Questions:

There are two questions I usually recommend asking after you've asked all of the job/company-related questions you have.

1). Ask if there's any other questions they have for you, or any more information you can provide?

Asking this question allows the interview to pause and consider if they have any lingering questions or any concerns that they feel you haven't adequately addressed. It also shows that you're meticulous and that you pay attention to details and you're eager to provide them with an accurate picture of yourself.

Example: *"Do you have any other questions for me? Or is there any other information I can provide you with that will prove to you I'm the best candidate?"*

This is both a challenge and a valid question. Most often, they'll just say, "Nothing that comes to mind." Or something like that, but there's a chance they will have some lingering question that hasn't gotten addressed yet and it could make all the difference in your interview.

2). Ask, "Is there anything you think that would prevent me from doing this job?"

This is a bit of an aggressive question and can be seen by some as a "soft close." You're basically asking them to tell you if they think you're a good candidate. Obviously, you should feel the interviewer out. After having completed the interview, you should be able to tell how a question like this might affect them. If they seem open-minded and positive, there isn't much of a risk in asking this question.

Example: "Based on my qualifications and our discussion here today, do you think I'm a good candidate for this job? Is there anything you see that would prevent me from excelling in this job?"

Or you could ask something like, "How do I compare to other candidates you've interviewed?"

You can tweak how you'd ask this question and make it more or less aggressive based on your gut feeling about the interview, but it's a great way to challenge the interviewer to tell you what he/she really thinks. There's a good chance they'll just give you a generic non-committal response like, "I think we've gotten a good idea of who you are and what your qualifications are" But there's always a chance that they may express some lingering concern that they feel disqualifies you from consideration for the job. You may or may not be able to alleviate that concern with further discussion. Most importantly, though, it shows the interviewer that you're direct, confident, and goal-oriented.

The 20 Second Wrap-up

In 20 seconds, reiterate why you're the best fit and re-state your immense interest in the company and the position. This is of paramount importance because, much like your vital first-impression with the interviewers, this could be your lasting impression with them. This is the message you want to leave them with, so make it count and cut out any minutia. Just stick to the 2 or 3 most important points that show why you're the ideal candidate for this job while also expressing your excitement and interest in the opportunity.

Next Steps:

Be sure to ask the interviewer about next steps in the process. You can say something like, "I'm interested in moving forward, so I'd like to know what the next steps are and what the timeline for your decision is."

Lastly, make sure you get the interviewer's contact information. You can say, "I'd like to stay in touch during the decision-making process, what's the best way to communicate with you?" It's likely they will either give you their card or their email address if they did not already do so at the beginning of the interview.

Part 5: Following up After the Interview

Thank you Email:

About 24 hours after your interview, you'll want to send a thank you email to everyone that was present at the interview. Keep the email short, pointed, and sincere. A general framework for your followup/thank you email follows:

- Thank them for their time and the opportunity to interview
- Tell them 1 or 2 things you really enjoyed learning about the company/job in the interview
- Very concisely restate why you're the best fit for the interview.
- Express your desire to move forward and your interest in the opportunity
- Thank them again and express your desire to hear back from them as soon as possible.

If you don't have the contact information of the people you interviewed with or if there were multiple interviewers and you didn't manage to obtain all of their email addresses, email the person who arranged the interview and ask them to forward it on to the interviewers for you. You can also ask the person who arranged the interview to give you the email address for the interviewers so you can send them a thank you email.

There is no excuse not to send a thank you email. Employers differ on the importance they place on thank you emails, but it's not uncommon for stellar candidates to lose the opportunity because they failed to send a follow-up email.

Follow Up:

After a reasonable amount of time has passed (1-2 weeks) you can and should send a follow-up email checking in with them. Do not worry about being annoying or nagging. Employers want someone who is assertive and a go-getter. You want to stay at the forefront of their mind and stand out in any way you can. Stick to the timeline they've set. If they say they'll be deciding within 2 weeks, wait at least 2 weeks before emailing them. You do run the risk of appearing overly aggressive or annoying if you email them before the timeline they gave you has elapsed.

Guidelines for the followup email:
- Keep it very short—a few sentences. This is not your opportunity to plead your case as a candidate. At this point, you've done everything you can to show that you're an awesome candidate. You just have to wait for and rely on their decision.
- Don't be aggressive. Keep it cordial and try to sound understanding of how busy they must be (even if in your head you're going crazy with impatience because you just want an answer).
- Don't automatically assume you didn't get the job. Be optimistic. If you haven't heard from them, assume they

haven't made their decision yet and that you're still in the running

- Be helpful. Ask if there's anything further you can do to assist them in the decision-making process.

Don't be afraid to continually send emails until you receive a response. Keep them reasonably spaced out and keep your tone cordial and non-aggressive. Your goal here is to build a relationship with the decision-maker. Even if you got passed over for this opportunity, there's a very good chance that they may have other opportunities arising in the very near future that you may be considered for.

Conclusion:

If you've made it this far in this book, then you should congratulate yourself. You're already miles ahead of most other people you'll be competing with for this job. You have the inside scoop. You have all the tools to adequately represent yourself and guarantee your best possible chance to get the job you really want.

Remember that contrary to popular belief, the best way to stand out is by ignoring the job application process altogether. Apply to a company—not a job. Find a company you really like, and ignore their job postings. Find a decision maker, and convince them that they simply have to have you on their team. It's a paradox that the best way to compete for a job is to not compete at all. Experts say that the absolute worst way to go after a job is by finding a job posting and applying for it. It will be so much harder to make real headway when you get lost in a sea of other applicants. Plus, your resume may never even get to the desk of a decision-maker.

When you apply for a job, your resume gets run through automated filtering programs that may take you out of the running for stupid reasons before your resume has even been seen by a human pair of eyes. You want to cut out all the unnecessary steps. Cut right to the chase. Find the decision-maker using the steps provided in this book, and convince them that you would be a valuable addition to their team. If the timing is right and you do a good job, the company will find a place for you—regardless of the public job postings they advertise.

With many of the skills and practices outlined in this book, practice makes perfect. You will become more and more comfortable with all of this the more you practice. Practice your interviewing skills with friends. Cold email companies you're not even interested in, just to cut your teeth. Before you know it, you will be able to face any employment hurdle with confidence. This confidence will become noticeable. Decision-makers will see it, they will want it, and suddenly— you will stand out. You will rise head and shoulders above the crowd.

23574746R00076

Made in the USA
San Bernardino, CA
27 January 2019